Published by:

FROM THE DRIVING SEAT

Thame, OX9 3WW, UK

www.fromthedrivingseat.com

ISBN: 978-1-3999-7834-7

Photography, design and layout by
Peter Osborne (pj.osborne@fromthedrivingseat.com)

Printed in England by
BCQ Group, Buckingham, UK

Other From The Driving Seat books:
MUD OR DUST - The Birth of UK Rallycross (Jeremy Walton & Peter Osborne)

Front cover photo:
HGPCA Gallett Trophy for Pre-1966 GP cars,
Silverstone Classic, July 28 2019
Left to right: Driver, Julian Bronson - Car, Scarab Offenhauser
Driver, Tony Wood - Car, Maserati TecMec
Driver, Tom Dark - Car, Cooper T51
Followed by a gaggle of mid-field runners

This page:
Marshals, the unsung heroes without whom no motorsport could take place, acknowledge finishing racers at The Silverstone Classic 2012.

INTRODUCTION

In *Classic Racing* we journey to Silverstone for the largest Classic racing event in the world. Originally the Silverstone Classic, renamed as Classic Silverstone in 2022, and now The Silverstone Festival, this unique event attracts thousands to the Home of British Motoring Racing over a long summer weekend.

For ten years from 2012, apart from 2014 (although results for that year are included), and 2020 when The Classic did not take place due to Covid lockdown, the author photographed at The Classic. Reports from these meetings by Jeremy Walton (2012-2015) and Peter Osborne (2016-2023) originally appeared on the fromthedrivingseat.com website. Those race reports plus the author's photographs and captions form the basis of this book in which we revisit the days when you could actually see drivers at work as they wrestled their, sometimes recalcitrant, charges around the track, as seen in this photo of Chris Phillips at the wheel of a 1953 Cooper Bristol during the Maserati Trophy race for pre-1966 GP Cars at the Silverstone Classic in 2016.

The photographs in this book, all taken by the author, illustrate the breadth of classic motorsport displayed at the Silverstone Classic between 2012 and 2023, from Historic Formula Junior to Historic Formula One —and everything in-between.

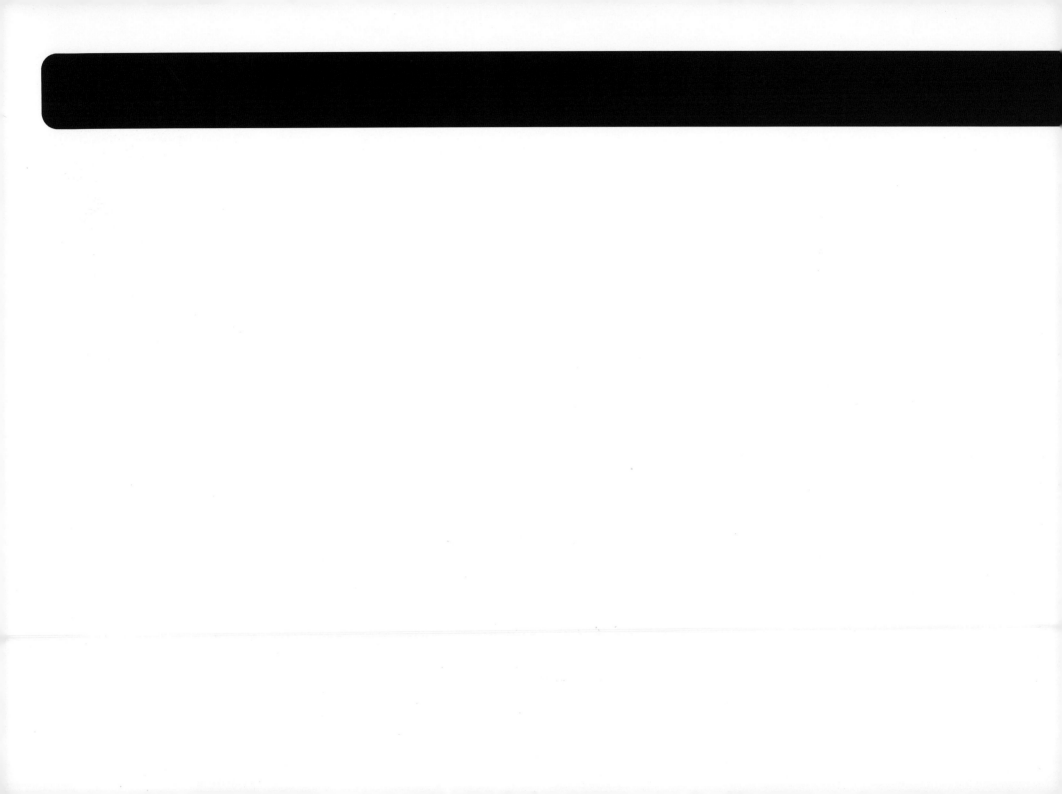

CONTENTS

FLYMO MONDEO!

Alan Strachan in the works 1995 Valvoline Team Mondeo goes grass cutting during the Super Touring Car Trophy race at the 2015 Silverstone Classic.

Andy Rouse Engineering ran the 1995 Auto Trader BTCC Ford works effort, with Paul Radisich and Kelvin Burt driving the V6 Mondeos.

SILVERSTONE CLASSIC 2018
START OF THE HISTORIC TOURING CAR CHALLENGE WITH TONY DRON TROPHY

FOREWORD

This unique book cuts to the chase, for surely it is motor racing in motion that attracts the eye and leads to the enjoyable post event chat: "Did you see that?" Well, Peter Osborne not only saw those spectacular moments, but lugged bulky cameras along to make sure such split second images were crisply and colourfully recorded, regardless of the erratic British weather!

Rather than present us with a general and shallow overview of the many classic events the UK hosts, from pub meets to major public attractions that attract more visitors than Grand Prix, Peter chose to focus sharply on Silverstone's remarkable brimming grids. Which means we gain a pictorial flavour, concise captions and results for the superb variety of vehicles lapping Silverstone's rapid curves.

Expect to view from Formula One of recent memory, through to sports racing and priceless pre-war machines, to touring cars of many shapes, and ages. Since those that drive these rare cars are also of different talent levels, also anticipate some bumpy interludes along the way!

Peter also has lens time for airborne classics and the atmosphere of these special Northamptonshire events — Enjoy!

JEREMY WALTON, Wiltshire January 2024

*Jeremy Walton is the author of 35 automotive books, many with classic themes.
Walton has either participated in motor sports or worked with Peter Osborne since 1968.*

Walton enjoys a parade lap at the Silverstone Classic

Kingsley Ingram in the orange 1998 Mazda 323F lifts a rear wheel into Brooklands corner in pursuit of the Dave Brodie Ford RS500, during the Fujifilm Touring Car Trophy race.

SILVERSTONE CLASSIC 2012

July 20th. – July 22nd.

Backed by the AA and emphasising more family attractions than previous editions, Silverstone got luckier with the fickle UK summer than at GP. Promoter-organisers Goose Communications reported a record 83,500 crowd to witness 24 races and some 7000 classic, and not so classic, vehicles on display. Silverstone Auctions revealed a £1.1 million take with an XK150 Jaguar leading the pack on £67,760.

Highlights of the weekend were the Saturday and Sunday runnings of the Daily Express International Trophy for Grand Prix Masters. In Saturday's race Michael Lyons (Hesketh 308E) led comfortably and set fastest lap until the car stopped on lap 8 before the race was red-flagged, handing the win to Bill Coombs (Tyrrell 009) with Steve Hartley's Arrows A4 taking the second spot and Michael Fitzgerald (Williams FW08) in third. Coombs and Hartley repeated the one-two in Sunday's race after coming under pressure from Michael Lyons who charged through the field from the twelfth row of the grid to challenge the leaders but had to settle for third at the flag.

Lyons had better luck in Saturday's previous Peter Gethin Trophy for F2 and F500 when he won in a Lola T400 after race leader Simon Hadfield (Trojan T101) spun, gifting the win to Lyons with Martin Stretton's March 742in second. Hadfield however triumphed in Sunday's running with Stretton again taking second while Lyons did not finish.

Tin-Top fans were rewarded with the Alan Mann Trophy race for under 2-litre Touring Cars on Saturday, and two races for the Fujifilm Touring Car Trophy 1970-2000. The Alan Mann Trophy saw a 1-2 Lotus Cortina finish with solo-driving Shaun McInerney taking the victory from the Leo Voyazides/Simon Hadfield Cortina, with the Banks' brothers Alfa Romeo Giulia Sprint GTA in third. After 50 minutes of racing just over 2 seconds covered the first three finishers.

Saturday's running of the Fujifilm Trophy saw Rick Pearson (Nissan Primera) set fastest lap and take the win from the Vauxhall Cavalier driven by Frank Wrathall, with Richard Hawken driving another Nissan Primera into third. These three repeated their finishing spots in Sunday's Fujifilm Trophy. In fact the first five finishers were the same as Saturday except that Neil Smith (Alfa Romeo 156) and Dave Jarman (Nissan Primera) who finished fourth and fifth respectively swapped positions on Sunday to finish fifth and fourth.

Saturday also saw the Classic Celebrity race featuring famous faces, including Sir Patrick Stewart and Heston Blumenthal, driving Morgan Lightweights. Pole sitter actor Kelvin Fletcher, famous for playing Andy Sugden in ITV soap *Emmerdale*, led from start to finish to win by over 7 seconds from musicians Brian Johnson and Jay Kay (Fletcher has since gone on to race in British Touring Car and British GT championships).

Other races over the weekend included two races for Historic Formula Junior which were won by Jon Milicevic (Cooper T59) and David Methley (Brabham BT6).

The Stirling Moss Trophy for pre-'61 sports cars saw a win for the Buncombe/Ward Lister Jaguar Costin, while the Young/Smith Cooper Jaguar T33 took the laurels in the Woodcote Trophy race for pre-'56 Sportscars.

Apart from the GP Masters races, there were other historic F1 races for both front engined pre-1961 GP cars and rear engined pre-1966 cars. The two pre-'66 races were won by Jason Minshaw in a Brabham BT4, while pre-'61 honours went to Philip Walker and Roger Wills both in Lotus 16's.

JDW

RAC WOODCOTE TROPHY

The Austin Healey 100M (#44) of Mike Thorne and Johnny Todd leads the Allard J2 (#57) of Verey/Welch, the Jaguar D-Type (#147) of Jonathan Bailey, Stephen Bond/Keith Fell silver Lister Bristol (#85), and the Frazer Nash Le Mans Replica (#20) driven by Martin Hunt and Patrick Blakeney-Edwards.

FUJIFILM TOURING CAR TROPHY

The 1983 BMW 635CSi driven by Jody Halse passes the year 2000 Ford Mondeo of Alvin Powell into Brooklands during the race on Sunday.

Hans Stuck drove this BMW for three rounds of the 1983 British Saloon Car Championship, in which Steve Soper finished top of the points table driving one of three TWR Rover Vitessses; but Frank Sytner lodged a protest about the Rovers and six months after the championship finished all three Rovers were disqualified with the title being awarded to Andy Rouse who had finished third in the points driving an Alfa Romeo GTV6.

2012

FUJIFILM TOURING CAR TROPHY

The 1977 Jaguar XJ-S of Richard Masters leaves a smoke screen for following drivers before retiring on lap seven.

Jaguar had a number of race wins with the XJ-S, firstly in the USA in the 1970s where Bob Tullius in his Group 44 prepared XJ-S won the 1978 Trans-Am drivers championship and took the manufacturers title for Jaguar.

In Europe Tom Walkinshaw won the 1984 European Touring Car Championship driving his TWR-prepared XJ-S.

FUJIFILM TOURING CAR TROPHY

Sunday's running of the race saw a race-long battle between the 1975 Zakspeed Ford Escort RS1800 of Mark Wright and the 1994 Vauxhall Cavalier of Mark Jones, with Wright taking ninth place from Jones by just over half a second at the flag.

In the 1994 BTCC the 16v Vauxhall Cavaliers were driven by John Cleland and Jeff Allam, with Cleland finishing fourth in the championship.

Zakspeed Escorts were very successful in the DRM (Deutsche Rennsport Meisterschaft) German Racing Championship winning the title in four successive years from 1973-1976 in the hands of Dieter Glemser and Hans Heyer.

2012

FUJIFILM TOURING CAR TROPHY

Mark Smith takes to the grass on the entry to Luffield during Sunday's Fujilfilm Touring Car Trophy in the BMW E30 M3.

Steve Soper drove this car in the 1992 German DTM for the Italian BMW M Team Bigazzi finishing ninth in the overall championship standings. He had finished fifth in the championship for the same team in the previous year.

FUJIFILM TOURING CAR TROPHY

Frank Wrathall drove this 1995 Vauxhall Cavalier to second in both runnings of the Fujilfilm Touring Car Trophy. Wrathall was the 2010 Ginetta G50 champion before moving on to the British Touring Car Championship in 2011, 2012 and 2013 driving a Toyota Avensis for his family-owned Dynojet Race Team.

The Fujifilm sponsored Cavalier was entered in the 1996 Autotrader BTCC by Mint Motorsport and driven by Richard Kaye, who's best result was eighth at Snetterton.

2012

FUJIFILM TOURING CAR TROPHY

Fourth and fifth in the two Fujifilm Touring Car Trophy races for Dave Jarman in this ex-Team Dynamics Nissan Primera, which competed in the 1998 and 1999 Autotrader BTCC series driven by Matt Neal. Neal won the Michelin Cup for independents and came ninth overall in 1999.

He also co-drove the Primera with Steve Richards to second place in the 1998 Bathurst 1000 at the Mount Panorama Circuit in Australia.

FUJIFILM TOURING CAR TROPHY

Michael Bell's "Lairy Canary" 1974 Ford Escort leads the 2000 Prodrive Ford Mondeo of Bernard Hogarth into Luffield during Sunday's running of the Fujifilm Touring Car Trophy.

They finished in reverse order with the Mondeo taking 24th spot just 1.3 seconds ahead of the Escort.

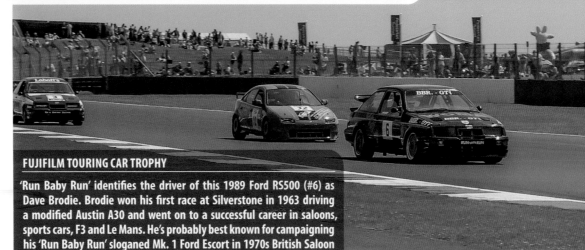

FUJIFILM TOURING CAR TROPHY

'Run Baby Run' identifies the driver of this 1989 Ford RS500 (#6) as Dave Brodie. Brodie won his first race at Silverstone in 1963 driving a modified Austin A30 and went on to a successful career in saloons, sports cars, F3 and Le Mans. He's probably best known for campaigning his 'Run Baby Run' sloganed Mk. 1 Ford Escort in 1970s British Saloon Car championships.

Here he is leading the 1995 Mazda 323F of Kingsley Ingram and the Labatts-liveried Ford RS500 of Paul Smith during Sunday's race.

2012

RAC TOURIST TROPHY

Jackie Oliver and Gary Pearson in this 1960 Ferrari 250 SWB looked set to win the Tourist Trophy from pole position until the car stopped a few laps from the end, handing the win to Nick Naismith's Aston Martin.

RAC TOURIST TROPHY

The thundering AC Cobra driven by Martin Hunt and Patrick Blakeney-Edwards took sixth place at the flag.

RAC TOURIST TROPHY

Julien and Matthew Draper qualified this Aston Martin DB4 GT Zagato on the third row of the grid alongside eventual winner Nick Naismith, and were running in fourth spot for the first few laps before retiring.

Italian coachbuilder Zagato produced this smaller, lighter, more aerodynamic (and better looking) version of the standard DB4, which was introduced at the 1960 London Motor Show. Its competition debut was at Goodwood at Easter 1961 when Stirling Moss drove into third place in the Fordwater Trophy race.

The May 1961 issue of *Motor Sport* in its report of the Goodwood Easter meeting described the Zagato as *".. may be lighter than a normal G.T. but its weight distribution has suffered and its road-holding, in consequence, has deteriorated."*

RAC TOURIST TROPHY

Winner of the RAC Tourist Trophy race Nick Naismith in the 1961 Aston Martin DB4 (#17) lines up coming out of Aintree corner to pass the Jaguar E-Type (#50) of Michael O'Shea and David Hall which finished in 17th place.

RAC WOODCOTE TROPHY

John Young and Andrew Smith shared driving duties to take this 1954 Cooper Jaguar T33 to second in the RAC Woodcote Trophy race on Saturday after the Gary and John Pearson Jaguar D-Type. Sunday's running saw the positions reversed with the Cooper taking the win from the Jaguar.

Peter Whitehead asked John Cooper to build a car for him that was lighter than the Jaguar C Type that he had been campaigning. Driving the resulting Cooper Jaguar T33 Whitehead's best result was a third place in Portugal behind the Lancias of Villoresi and Castolletti.

Whitehead's career highlights included winning the Le Mans 24 Hours in 1951 (works Jaguar C Type with Peter Walker), and coming second at the 1958 Le Mans (Aston Martin DB3S with his half-brother Graham Whitehead). Later the same year he was killed when the Mk. 1 Jaguar 3.4 saloon in which he was co-driving with Graham left the road during the Tour de France.

RAC WOODCOTE TROPHY

The Maserati 300S (#33) driven by Conrad Ulrich and Willy Green leads the Williams/Skipworth Jaguar D-Type (#32), Verey/Walch Allard J2 (#57), Woolmer/Darcey Austin Healey 100S (#29), and Anthony Galliers-Pratt in the Frazer Nash Targa Florio (#52) into Luffield corner.

The Maserati 300S made its World Sportscar Championship debut at the 1955 Sebring 12 Hour race where privateers Bill Spear/Sherwood Johnstone finished third ahead of the works 300S driven by Valezano/Pardisa. In 1956 Maserati hired Stirling Moss who, with Carlos Menditéguy, won the opening round of the WSC at Buenos Aires. Another works 300S driven by Behra/González finished third.

RAC WOODCOTE TROPHY

Andrew Sharp drove this Aston Martin DB2 in the Woodcote Trophy race for Pre-1956 sportscars.

At the first post-war Le Mans 24 Hour race in 1949, Aston Martin entered three pre-production DB2s, one with a 2.5 litre six cylinder Lagonda engine to be driven by Charles Brackenbury and Leslie Johnson and two using the Aston Martin 2 litre 4 cylinder engine with the driver pairings of Arthur Jones/Nick Haines and 'TASO' Mathieson/Pierre Maréchal.

After only a few laps the Lagonda engined car was retired after overheating and requiring a water top-up before it was allowed under the regulations. Early on the Sunday afternoon Maréchal, who had been running strongly in fourth, albeit with fading brakes, crashed at Maison Blanche suffering serious injuries from which he died the following day. The Jones/Haines car finished the race in seventh place.

In 1950 Aston Martin returned to Le Mans with a full works team managed by John Wyer. Three 2.6 litre DB2s driven by George Abacassis/Lance Macklin, RegParnell/Charles Brackenbury, and Eric Thompson/John Gordon took the start. The Thompson/Gordon car completed only eight laps before the engine called enough; but Abecassis/Macklin finished fifth, with Parnell/Brackenbury in sixth securing a 1-2 in class for Aston Martin.

RAC WOODCOTE TROPHY

In 1955 the US magazine *Road & Track* wrote that: *"Frank Kurtis of Glendale, California, deserves full credit for being the first man in America to attempt to produce an American production sports car..."*. After World War Two Kurtis cars dominated the midget racing scene in the USA, and over the next 20 years the Kurtis Kraft company built over 500 midgets, mostly with Offenhauser power.

The midget success gave the company the wherewithal to design and enter cars for the Indianapolis 500 in 1948, winning the race with Johnnie Parsons in 1950 following that with wins in 1951, 1953, 1954 and 1955.

The Kurtis 500, which was produced in various forms from 1953, was basically a two-seat, road-legal version of Kurtis Kraft's Indy cars. This 1954 Kurtis 500S was driven in the Woodcote Trophy by Adam and Joe Singer.

Race 1: **Historic Formula Junior**
First: Jon Milicevic (Cooper T59)
Second: Sam Wilson (Cooper T59)
Third: David Methley (Brabham BT6)

Race 2: **Peter Gethin Trophy for F2 & F5000**
First: Michael Lyons (Lola T400)
Second: Martin Stretton (March 742
Third: Simon Hadfield (Trojan T101

Race 3: **Alan Mann Trophy for Under 2-litre Touring Cars**
First: McInerney (Ford Lotus Cortina)
Second: Voyazides/Hadfield (Ford Lotus Cortina)
Third: Banks/Banks (Alfa Romeo Giulia Sprint GTA)

Race 4: **Stirling Moss Trophy for Pre-1961 Sports Cars**
First: Buncombe/Ward (Lister Jaguar Costin)
Second: Dodd/Dodd (Cooper Monaco T49)
Third: McIntyre / McIntyre (Lotus 15)

Race 5: **Daily Express International Trophy for GP Masters**
First: Bill Coombs (Tyrrell 009)
Second: Steve Hartley (Arrows A4)
Third: Michael Fitzgerald (Williams FW08)

Race 6: **HGPCA Pre-1966 Rear Engine GP Cars**
First: Jason Minshaw (Brabham BT4)
Second: John Harper (Brabham BT4)
Third: Rod Jolley (Cooper T45/51)

Race 7: **Masters 'Gentleman Drivers' Pre-1966 GT**
First: Minshaw/Stretton (Jaguar E-Type)
Second: Voyazides/Hadfield (AC Cobra)
Third: Pearson (Jaguar E-Type)

Race 8: **Jaguar E-Type Challenge**
First: Alex Buncombe (Jaguar E-Type)
Second: Jason Minshaw (Jaguar E-Type)
Third: Jon Minshaw (Jaguar E-Type)

Race 9: **HGPCA Pre-1961 Front Engine GP Cars**
First: Philip Walker (Lotus 16 368)
Second: Roger Wills (Lotus 16 363)
Third: Eddie McGuire (Lotus 16 362)

Race 10: **Fujifilm Touring Car Trophy 1970-2000**
First: Rick Pearson (Nissan Primera)
Second: Frank Wrathall (Vauxhall Cavalier)
Third: Richard Hawken (Nissan Primera)

Race 11: **Silverstone Classic Celebrity Challenge**
First: Kelvin Fletcher (Morgan Lightweight)
Second: Brian Johnson (Morgan Lightweightt)
Third: Jay Kay (Morgan Lightweightt

Race 12: **RAC Woodcote Trophy for pre-1956 Sports Cars**
First: Pearson/Pearson (Jaguar D-Type)
Second: Young/Smith (Cooper Jaguar T33)
Third: Webb/Reid (Jaguar C-Type)

Race 13: **Group C Endurance Race Cars**
First: Gareth Evans (Mercedes C9)
Second: Roger Wills (Lancia LC2)
Third: Chris D'Ansembourg (Porsche 962)

Race 14: **Historic Formula Junior**
First: David Methley (Brabham BT6)
Second: Sam Wilson (Cooper T59)
Third: Andrew Hibberd (Lotus 22

Race 15: **Peter Gethin Trophy for F2 & F5000**
First: Simon Hadfield (Trojan T101)
Second: Martin Stretton (March 742)
Third: Neil Fowler (March 75)

Race 16: **RAC Woodcote Trophy for pre-1956 Sports Cars**
First: Young/Smith (Cooper Jaguar T33)
Second: Pearson/Pearson (Jaguar D-Type)
Third: Webb/Reid (Jaguar C-Type)

RAC WOODCOTE TROPHY
The 1951 Frazer Nash Mille Miglia of Philip Champion and Sam Stretton spins, and recovers, at Brooklands.

Race 17: RAC Tourist Trophy for Historic Cars (Pre-1963 GT)
First: Naismith/Young (Aston Martin DB4)
Second: Ben Adams (Turner Mk2)
Third: Friedrichs/Clark (Aston Martin DP212)

Race 18: HGPCA Pre-1961 Front Engine GP Cars
First: Roger Wills (Lotus 16 363)
Second: Philip Walker (Lotus 16 368)
Third: Eddie McGuire (Lotus 16 362)

Race 19: Fujifilm Touring Car Trophy 1970-2000
First: Rick Pearson (Nissan Primera)
Second: Frank Wrathall (Vauxhall Cavalier)
Third: Richard Hawken (Nissan Primera)

Race 20: Daily Express International Trophy for GP Masters
First: Bill Coombs (Tyrrell 009)
Second: Steve Hartley (Arrows A4)
Third: Michael Lyons (Hesketh 308E)

Race 21: Group C Endurance Race Cars
First: Gareth Evans (Mercedes C9)
Second: Nicholas Minassian (Lancia LC2)
Third: Herve Regout (Porsche 962)

Race 22: World Sports Car Masters
First: Smith/Bryant (Lola T70)
Second: Knapfield/Stretton (Ferrari 312PB)
Third: Tandy (Lola T70 Mk3b)

Race 23: HGPCA Pre-1966 Rear Engine GP Cars
First: Jason Minshaw (Brabham BT4)
Second: John Harper (Brabham BT4)
Third: Rod Jolley (Cooper T45/51)

Race 24: Jaguar E-Type Challenge
First: Alex Buncombe (Jaguar E-Type)
Second: Gregor Fisken (Jaguar E-Type)
Third: John Pearson (Jaguar E-Type)

Ford Lotus Cortina, Fiat Abarth 1000TC and Alfa Romeo Giulia power through the heat haze away from Copse Corner in the Sir John Whitmore Trophy for Under 2-litre Touring Cars.

SILVERSTONE CLASSIC 2013

July 26th. – July 28th.

Bigger and better, Silverstone's 3-day classic racing weekend attracted over 90,000 spectators plus 1,113 racing entries from exotic to eccentric and over 9,000 classic and current cars on display, most coming from the 80 motor clubs who turned out in force.

As you'd expect the club parades of the full GP circuit as used for the 24 races were also packed, notably by 1,208 Porsche 911s reaching 50 years in production and Aston Martin doubling that with their centenary, albeit scarcely on Porsche's scale.

Although the racing was fabulous — particularly our favourite touring cars from three different eras and capacities from 1 to 7 litres — chief sponsors the AA do add a family sideshows element to the weekend.

BMW also got a lot more serious, providing a mini-millennium wheel for public and their (fast-track) owners, their two story hospitality/showroom building surrounded by a sea of classic to current product.

A welcome personality in attendance was a recovering (from a broken pelvis) Murray Walker, the much loved commentator, a former owner of BMWs two and four-wheeled.

Silverstone like to promote the 'Rocking and Racing' theme to take over the trackside evenings with a sound stage that would not look out of place at a major open air concert. This year the bands included the *Hollies* and tribute performers marking *Eagles* and *Stone Roses* territory.

On an unexpectedly sunny Saturday, the racing highlights included former triple World Touring Car Champ Andy Priaulx holding off the Lotus Cortina horde in the Sir John Whitmore Trophy race for under 2-litre touring cars for much of his opening stint in the Laranca BMW 1800TiSA which he shared with Richard Solomons, although final victory went to the Lotus Cortina of Leo Voyazides and Simon Hadfield.

Former BTCC/Porsche series Champion Tim Harvey in a Ford RS500 got the jump on the Saturday Super Touring crowd and actually led for the opening laps against a generation of later front-drive 2-litres; but had to settle for second at the flag to the Vauxhall Cavalier GSi of BTCC Toyota ace, Frank Wrathall, who also took the win in Sunday's race.

There was also a sweet-sounding 3.4 litre Ford Capri that had sensational acceleration. Plus more diversity than we ever enjoyed back in the day with two V12 Jags, Alfa 156s, Nissan Primeras, and even a MG Metro Turbo.

So, was Silverstone simply marvellous and we should forget the alternative twin attractions of Goodwood Revival and Festival?

No, they are very different. Silverstone is a foot-punishing sprawl with the accent on size in acreage and exhibits. Both have fantastic racing, with Goodwood having the quality cachet and Silverstone the slick pace and the sheer numbers of race and performance hardware — more than Goodwood wants to accommodate.

Silverstone is also more interactive with its spectators and club supporters, so you can participate in parades or trackside experiences galore.

We originally took a BMW or a Sprite and enjoyed the parade laps with hundreds of others, just being a club member or a participant on a classic road route being sufficient qualification over the money and class-conscious themes of dress-up Goodwood.

However, there were aspects of Silverstone's event that fell well below Goodwood standards, most obviously the twin, then solo, Spitfire air display on Saturday. Past Silverstones have featured more variety and a diversity beyond the default Spitfire aerobics.

JDW

2013

Unmistakeable sight and sound of Spitfires graced the sky above Silverstone

SIR JOHN WHITMORE TROPHY

The Tomlin/Stretton Lotus Cortina (#16) leading this group locked the right front wheel on almost every lap on the entry to Copse during the Sir John Whitmore Trophy race for under 2-litre Touring Cars on Sunday.

Mixing it with the Lotus Cortinas is the BMW 1800 Ti of Clark/McCaig. They finished in this order, the Ford in sixth and the BMW seventh.

SIR JOHN WHITMORE TROPHY

The Leo Voyazides/Simon Hadfield Lotus Cortina secured pole for the Sir John Whitmore Trophy race and, after falling back through the field mid-race, came back strongly in the last few laps to take the win at the flag.

SIR JOHN WHITMORE TROPHY

The first of the Alfas to finish in this race for under 2 litre touring cars was this 1965 Giulia Sprint GTA driven by Neil Merry who crossed the line in 17th place.

SIR JOHN WHITMORE TROPHY

Nick Swift took the Swiftune prepared Mini Cooper S to a strong tenth place, the first of the Minis to finish.

Voted the second most influential car of the 20th Century (after the Model T Ford) Alec Issigonis' innovative little car was introduced in 1959, and almost all compact cars since have adopted its front wheel drive, transverse engine layout.

Sir John Whitmore won the 1961 British Saloon Car Championship driving a Mini. John Cooper persuaded BMC management to produce a performance variant, the Mini Cooper, featuring a larger displacement engine (997cc over 848cc), twin carburettors and front disc brakes, which appeared in late 1961. In 1962 John Love won the British Saloon Car Championship driving a Mini Cooper, with Minis winning the same championship in 1969 (Alec Poole, Cooper S), 1978 and 1979 (Richard Longman, 1275 GT).

BMC's Competition Department at Abingdon prepared Minis for rallying under the direction of Stuart Turner, famously winning the Monte Carlo Rally in 1964, 1965 and 1967, and would have won in 1966 as well had they not been controversially disqualified over a headlamp irregularity.

SIR JOHN WHITMORE TROPHY

Almost the polar opposite of the Mini is the Fiat 600 and its many derivatives with in-line engines mounted at the back driving the rear wheels, as in this Fiat Abarth 1000TC driven by Jasper Izaks and Geoff Turral who did not finish but recorded the fastest lap in their class.

Carlo Abarth was a successful motorbike racer in the 1920s who founded his eponymously named company in Bologna in 1949 in partnership with Armando Scagliarini initially producing exhaust systems.

When Fiat introduced the 600 in 1955 Abarth realised the performance potential of these little cars and produced a number of modified versions, with their signature propped open engine covers, supposedly to help engine cooling; but actually to improve aerodynamics.

Abarth 1000TCs dominated their class in the European Touring Car Challenge in the mid 1960s winning the Division One driver's and manufacturer's titles in 1965, 1966 and 1967.

SIR JOHN WHITMORE TROPHY

Henry Mann in the iconic red and gold livery of the Alan Mann Racing Lotus Cortina leads the Alfa Romeo Giulia Sprint of Neil Merry and the Lotus Cortinas driven by Graham Wilson and Andy Wolfe past the National Pits.

SIR JOHN WHITMORE TROPHY

Andy Priaulx took the Laranaca Engineering BMW 1800Ti to a solid fifth place in the Sir John Whitmore Trophy. Here pursued by the Mike Gardiner/Phil Keen Lotus Cortina which did not finish.

STIRLING MOSS TROPHY

Alan and Jason Minshaw drove this Maserati Tipo 61 'Birdcage' to fourth spot in the Stirling Moss Trophy race for pre-1961 Sports Cars, fittingly as the preceding Tipo 60 model won its debut race in the hands of Stirling.

The T60/61 used a unique tubular space frame chassis made up of 200 small-diameter steel tubes welded together to make a cage like structure, resulting in a light but very rigid chassis. To overcome new Le Mans rules demanding a deeper windscreen Maserati recessed the base of the windscreen into the bodywork revealing the chassis tubes structure through the screen, immediately earning it the nickname 'Birdcage'.

Although fast and competitive, reliability problems plagued the cars in period with drivetrain failures forcing many retirements.

2013

STIRLING MOSS TROPHY

Tony Bianchi and Nick Wigley took Bianchi's Allard Farrallac to a solid mid-field finish.

Developed by Allard's for amateur racer Don Farrell in 1958, the one-off Farrallac utilised the chassis of the ex-Peter Collins cycle-winged Allard J2 with new enveloping bodywork and powered by a 6.4 litre Cadillac V8 engine.

Sydney Allard achieved the unique feat of a podium place at Le Mans (1950) and winning the Monte Carlo Rally (1952), both in a car bearing his own name. Allard cars achieved significant success in the late 1940s and early 1950s, including a Cadillac-engined model driven by Carroll Shelby (perhaps an early influence for his later Cobra?).

STIRLING MOSS TROPHY

A touch of opposite lock around Copse for the Arif/Young Austin Healey 100S during the Stirling Moss Trophy race.

These limited edition aluminium bodied racing variants of the Austin Healey 100 were hand built at the Donald Healey Motor Company in Warwick and given the 'S' designation after a third place finish and class win at the 1954 Sebring 12 hour race for a prototype driven by Lance Macklin and George Huntoon.

One of the first cars to feature disc brakes all round, the 100S enjoyed significant race victories during the middle 1950s.

2013

STIRLING MOSS TROPHY

British motor racing royalty from Aston Martin and Jaguar. The Aston Martin DBR1 of Friedrichs/Hadfield (#7) together with the Jaguar D-Type of Eastick/Quinn (#9) that finished 21st and 18th respectively in the Stirling Moss Trophy race.

Aston Martin and Jaguar both won the Le Mans 24 hour race in the 1950s, once for Aston Martin with the DBR1 in 1959, and five times for Jaguar with the C-Type and D-Type between 1951 and 1957.

STIRLING MOSS TROPHY

Jim Tester exits the National Pits in the Jaguar XK120. Introduced at the 1948 London Motor Show, with the first production model delivered to Hollywood legend Clark Gable, the XK120 was at the time the fastest production car in the world with a top speed of 120mph, hence the name.

Almost immediately successful on track the XK120 scored a 1-2 victory in the Daily Express One Hour Production Car race at Silverstone in August 1949 in the hands of Leslie Johnson and Peter Walker.

The XK 120 was equally at home rallying, winning the 1950 Alpine Rally driven by Ian Appleyard and navigated by his wife Pat (daughter of Sir William Lyons, the founder of Jaguar). The pair repeated the feat in 1951 and finished fourth in 1952.

STIRLING MOSS TROPHY

Accelerating out of the National Pits after the mandatory pit stop and driver change during the Stirling Moss Trophy race is the Smith/Ward Lister Costin which finished in second place and recorded the fastest lap of the race.

Brian Lister hired Frank Costin to create a replacement for the Lister 'Knobbly' with a more aerodynamic body and a lightweight spaceframe chassis. The new car made its debut in 1958, and in the 1959 Sebring 12 Hour race Stirling Moss and Ivor Bueb qualified the car second on the grid and were running strongly until disqualified for illegal refuelling.

TRANS-ATLANTIC TROPHY

Mike Whitaker/Nigel Reuben Ford Mustang (#46) leads the battle-scared Desmond Smail/Rob Huff Mini Cooper (#47). They finished seventh and ninth respectively in the first race of the Trans-Atlantic Trophy.

Introduced in 1964 the Mustang was an instant sales success for Ford selling over 400,000 in the first year. Its first appearance on track was as the pace car for the 1964 Indy 500 driven by Ford Motor Company Vice-President and Henry Ford's grandson, Benson Ford. In the same year Alan Mann Racing Mustangs took first and second place in the Touring Car category of the Tour de France Automobile driven by the driver pairings of Peter Procter/Andrew Cowan and Peter Harper/David Pollard respectively.

2013

TRANS-ATLANTIC TROPHY

Winner of the first of the Trans-Atlantic Trophy races, the Ford Falcon (#1) of Leo Voyazides and Simon Hadfield, leads third place finisher, the Mike Gardiner/Phil Keen Ford Falcon Sprint (#37) and the Ford Mustang (#6) of Henry Mann which finished in second place. Voyazides/Hadfield and Mann repeated those positions in the second race on Sunday, in which Wills/Panayiotou brought their Mercury Comet Cyclone into third.

An Alan Mann Racing prepared Falcon took Frank Gardner to victory in the 1967 British Saloon Car Championship.

2013

TRANS-ATLANTIC TROPHY

The Ford Mustang of Simon Miller and the Lotus Cortina of Norwegian pairing Viggo Lund and Martin Strommen sidelined after a coming together at Brooklands.

2013

TRANS-ATLANTIC TROPHY

Monstrous Ford Galaxie driven by Bill Shepherd dwarfs the hustling Minis behind.

The 7 litre Ford Galaxie burst on to the British Saloon Car racing scene when John Willment entered a Holman & Moody prepared 'lightweight' Galaxie at Silverstone in May 1963 driven by "Gentleman" Jack Sears, who had won the inaugural British Saloon Car Championship in 1958 driving an equally unlikely looking racer, an Austin A105 Westminster (inset). Sears won that 1963 Silverstone race with ease and went on to win the 1963 Championship driving the Galaxie, a Ford Cortina GT, and a Ford Lotus Cortina.

Galaxies were also driven in the 1963 Championship by illustrious F1 stars such as Graham Hill, Dan Gurney and Jack Brabham, with Gurney and Brabham both taking wins. In the 1964 season Galaxies continued to dominate, winning practically every race, but with different drivers, thereby handing the driver's title to a consistent Jim Clark in the Team Lotus Cortina.

Jack Sears' 1958 British Saloon Car Championship winning Austin Westminster at the 2018 Silverstone Classic BTCC 60th anniversary celebration.

SUPER TOURING CAR TROPHY

Neil Smith qualified this Alfa Romeo 156 on the third row of the grid for the Super Touring Car Trophy on Saturday and came through to take the lead and finish at the head of the field only to be excluded for "causing an avoidable incident".

Ex-F1 driver Stefano Modena drove this car in the 1998 and 1999 German Super Tourenwagen Cup for the Italian Euroteam. Since then the car was driven by Niklas Karlsonn in the Swedish Touring Car Championship.

SUPER TOURING CAR TROPHY

The Rover P6 with a 4.3 litre Traco-modified Oldsmobile engine recorded some successes for the British Leyland Competitions Department in the hands of Roy Pierpoint during the 1970 UK Group 2 Saloon Car championship.

Notably the car also easily led the 1970 Marathon de la Route (a gruelling 86 hour slog around the full 28.3 Km. Nürburgring circuit) driven by Pierpoint, Roger Enerver, and Clive Baker before an out of balance propshaft forced its retirement after 16 hours. Shortly afterwards Lord Stokes pulled the plug on the Abingdon-based operation, thereby ceasing all development work on the P6 racer although privateers continued to campaign the cars in UK club racing.

Unfortunately no such success in 2013 at Silverstone where the car, driven by Ian Giles, retired on the second lap of Saturday's Super Touring Car Trophy and did not appear for Sunday's race.

2013

Diminutive Honda Civic Type R of Martin Johnson about to be devoured by the heavy metal of Paul Pochiol's Broadspeed Jaguar XJ12 and the BMW E30 M3 of Mark Smith in Saturday's Super Touring Car Trophy race.

The Jaguar was 13th at the flag, while the Honda finished in last place. Mark Smith however was out of luck, retiring the BMW on lap 2.

The Type R derivative was introduced in 2001 with the seventh generation (EP3) of Honda's best selling Civic. Type R Civics were manufactured in Honda's Swindon factory for the UK and European markets. A Japanese domestic market (JDM) version, with a more track-oriented specification, was also assembled in Swindon and shipped to Japan.

In 2019 the 750 Motor club launched the *Type R Trophy*, a relatively low-cost single make championship featuring EP3 Generation Honda Type R cars with minimal modifications.

Winner of both Super Touring Car Trophy races, Frank Wrathall in the Vauxhall Cavalier (#11) follows the Ford Sierra RS500 Cosworth of Tim Harvey around The Loop during Saturday's race. Harvey took second place at the flag, 23.7 seconds behind Wrathall.

Tim Harvey previously drove the Andy Rouse prepared Labatt's RS500 in the 1989 British Touring Car Championship, winning two rounds and coming seventh in the overall championship.

2013

Stewart Whyte finished eighth in this Honda Accord in Saturday's running of the Super Touring Car Trophy, and second behind Frank Wrathall's winning Vauxhall Cavalier in the Sunday race.

Honda entered the British Touring Car Championship for the first time in 1996 with a two Accords driven by David Leslie and James Kaye. After a disappointing start to the season, Leslie won a support race at the British GP, plus two further wins to secure fourth in the championship.

Nick Swift in the MG Metro Turbo is tail-end Charlie at the start of Saturday's Super Touring Car Trophy race.

The MG Metro Turbo made its track debut at the Brands Hatch round of the 1983 British Saloon Car Championship driven by Tony Pond, but did not finish due to a gearbox problem.

At the last race of that season at Silverstone three cars were entered for Pond, Patrick Watts and Martin Brundle; but all finished in the last three places after having to pit with tyre trouble.

Despite a few class wins in 1984 Austin Rover withdrew from the BSCC at the end of the season in protest at how technical infringements were handled.

RACE RESULTS Silverstone Classic 2013

Race 1: **Peter Arundell Trophy for Historic Formula Junior**
First: *Andrew Hibberd (Lotus 22)*
Second: *Sam Wilson (Lotus 20/22)*
Third: *Jon Millicevic (Cooper T59)*

Race 2: **Balvenie Trophy for Historic Formula Ford**
First: *Callum Macleod (Merlyn Mk20)*
Second: *Sam Mitchell (Merlyn Mk20)*
Third: *Ben Simms (Jomo JMR7)*

Race 3: **Stirling Moss Trophy for Pre 1961 Sportscars**
First: *Bryant/Bryant (Lotus 15)*
Second: *Smith/Ward (Lister Costin)*
Third: *Walker/Wright (Lotus 15)*

Race 4: **Sir John Whitmore Trophy for Under 2 Litre Touring Cars**
First: *Voyazides/Hadfield (Ford Lotus Cortina)*
Second: *Meaden/Tromans (Ford Lotus Cortina Mk1)*
Third: *Mark Jones (Ford Lotus Cortina Mk1)*

Race 5: **FIA Masters Historic Formula One**
First: *Michael Lyons (RAM Williams FW07)*
Second: *Joaquin Folch (Brabham BT49C)*
Third: *Christophe D'Ansembourg (Williams FW07C)*

Race 6: **Trans-Atlantic Touring Car Trophy**
First: *Voyazides/Hadfield (Ford Falcon)*
Second: *Henry Mann (Ford Mustang)*
Third: *Gardiner/Keen (Ford Falcon Sprint)*

Race 7: **Froilan Gonzalez Trophy for HGPCA Pre'61 Grand Prix Cars**
First: *Julian Bronson (Scarab Offenhause)r*
Second: *Tony Smith (Ferrari 246 Dino 0007)*
Third: *Tony Wood (Maserati TecMec)*

Race 8: **FIA Masters Historic Sports Cars**
First: *Voyazides/Hadfield (Lola Mk3b)*
Second: *Steve Tandy (Lola T70 Mk3b)*
Third: *Monteverde/Pearson (Porsche 91)7*

Race 9: **The Peter Gethin Trophy for Formula 5000 and Formula 2 cars**
First: *Michael Lyons (Lola T400)*
Second: *Lee Dwyer (Lola T400)*
Third: *Neil Glover (Lola T330/332)*

Race 10: **Super Touring Car Trophy**
First: *Frank Wrathall (Vauxhall Cavalier)*
Second: *Tim Harvey (Ford Sierra RS500 Cosworth)*
Third: *Craig Davies (Ford RS500)*

Race 11: **Jim Clark Trophy for HGPCA Pre '66 GP Cars**
First: *Jason Minshaw (Brabham BT4)*
Second: *Jonathon Hughes (Cooper T53)*
Third: *Peter Horsman (Lotus 18/21 P1)*

Race 12: **Piper Heidsieck International Trophy for Pre '66 GT Cars**
First: *Pearson/Pearson (Jaguar E-Type)*
Second: *Voyazides/Hadfield (AC Cobra)*
Third: *Edward Morris (Lotus Elan)*

ASTON MARTIN OWNERS CLUB ON DISPLAY
AT THE 2013 SILVERSTONE CLASSIC

Race 13: Group C Endurance
CANCELLED DUE TO HEAVY RAIN

Race 14: Balvenie Trophy for Historic Formula Ford
First: Callum Macleod (Merlyn Mk20)
Second: Callum Grant (Merlyn Mk20a)
Third: Sam Mitchell (Merlyn Mk20)

Race 15: RAC Woodcote Trophy for Pre'56 Sports Cars
First: Pearson/Pearson (Jaguar D-Type)
Second: Young/Ward (Jaguar C-Type)
Third: Smith/Young (Cooper Jaguar T33)

Race 16: Peter Arundell Trophy for Historic Formula Junior
First: Sam Wilson (Lotus 20/22)
Second: Andrew Hibberd (Lotus 22)
Third: Jon Millicevic (Cooper T59)

Race 17: RAC Tourist Trophy for Historic Cars (Pre '63 GT)
First: Pearson/Oliver (Ferrari 250 SWB)
Second: Friedrichs/Hadfield (Aston Martin DP212)
Third: Cottingham/Smith (Jaguar E-Type)

Race 18: Group C
First: Nic Minassian (Jaguar XJR14)
Second: Gareth Evans (Mercedes C11)
Third: Steve Tandy (Nissan R90CK)

Race 19: Froilan Gonzalez Trophy for HGPCA Pre'61 Grand Prix Cars
First: Julian Bronson (Scarab Offenhauser)
Second: Tony Wood (Maserati TecMec)
Third: Rod Jollay (Lister Jaguar Monzanapolis)

Race 20: Super Touring Car Trophy
First: Frank Wrathall (Vauxhall Cavalie)r
Second: Stewart Whyte (Honda Accord)
Third: Craig Davies (Ford RS500)

Race 21: FIA Masters Historic Formula One
First: Michael Lyons (RAM Williams FW07)
Second: Joaquin Folch (Brabham BT49C)
Third: Steve Hartley (Arrows A4)

Race 22: Trans-Atlantic Touring Car Trophy
First: Voyazides/Hadfield (Ford Falcon)
Second: Henry Mann (Ford Mustang)
Third: Wills/Panayiotou (Mercury Comet Cyclone)

Race 23: Jim Clark Trophy for HGPCA Pre '66 GP Cars
First: Jason Minshaw –(Brabham BT4)
Second: Miles Griffiths (Cooper T51)
Third: Jonathon Hughes (Cooper T53)

Race 24: The Peter Gethin Trophy for Formula 5000 and Formula 2 cars
First: Michael Lyons (Lola T400)
Second: Lee Dwyer (March 782)
Third: Mark Dwyer (March 742)

RACE RESULTS Silverstone Classic 2014

Due to circumstances beyond their control the author did not attend the 2014 Silverstone Classic.
Although unable to report on and photograph the meeting the 2014 race results are included here.

Race 1: Peter Arundell Trophy for Historic Formula Junior
First: Sam Wilson (Lotus 20/22)
Second: Jon Milicevic (Cooper T59)
Third: Michael Hibberd (Lotus 27)

Race 2: Brian Henton Trophy for Classic Formula 3
First: Nick Padmore (March 783)
Second: Martin Stretton (Martini MK39)
Third: David Shaw (March 803B)

Race 3: Sir John Whitmore Trophy for Under 2 Litre Touring Cars
First: Meaden/Thomas (Ford Lotus Cortina)
Second: Brown/Dutton (Ford Lotus Cortina)
Third: Banks/Banks (Alfa Romeo Giulia Sprint GTA)

Race 4: Stirling Moss Trophy for pre-1961 Sports Cars
First: Minshaw/Keen (Lister Jaguar Knobbly)
Second: Ward (Lister Jaguar Costin)
Third: Leventis/Verdon-Roe (Ferrari 246S)

Race 5: FIA Masters Historic Formula One
First: Ollie Hancock (Fittipaldi F5A)
Second: Martin Stretton (Tyrrell 012)
Third: Christophe D'Ansembourg (Williams FW07/C)

Race 6: Jet Super Touring Car Trophy
First: James Dodd (Honda Accord)
Second: Stewart Whyte (Honda Accord)
Third: John Cleland (Vauxhall Vectra)

Race 7: Chopard International Trophy for pre-1966 GT Cars
First: McInerney (TVR Griffith)
Second: Kinch (Jaguar E-Type)
Third: Scragg/Nicoll-Jones (Jaguar E-Type)

Race 8: Jack Brabham Memorial Trophy for HGPCA pre-1966 GP Cars
First: Jason Minshaw (Brabham BT4)
Second: Jon Farley (Brabham BT11)
Third: Peter Horsman (Lotus 18/21 P1)

Race 9: Mustang Celebration Trophy
First: Leo Voyazides (Ford Falcon)
Second: Mike Gardiner (Ford Falcon)
Third: Tom Roche (Ford Mustang)

Race 10: Maserati Centenary Trophy for HGPCA pre-1961 GP Cars
First: Philip Walker (Lotus 16)
Second: Julian Bronson (Scarab Offenhauser)
Third: Tony Wood (TecMec Maserati F415)

Race 11: FIA Masters Historic Sports Cars
First: Voyazides/Hadfield (Lola T70 Mk3B)
Second: Wright/Wolfe (Lola T70 Mk3B)
Third: Harris/Meaden (Lola T70 Mk3B)

Race 12; Group C Endurance
First: Bob Berridge (Mercedes C11)
Second: Katsu Kubota (Nissan R90CK)
Third: Mike Donovan (Spice SE88)

Race 13: Brian Henton Trophy for Classic Formula 3
First: Nick Padmore (March 783)
Second: Martin Stretton (Martini MK39)
Third: David Shaw (March 803B)

Race 14: RAC Woodcote Trophy for pre-1956 Sports Cars
First: Wakeman/Blakeney-Edwards (Cooper T38)
Second: Pearson/Pearson (Jaguar D-Type)
Third: Owen/Knill-Jones (Kurtis 500S)

Race 15: Peter Arundell Trophy for Historic Formula Junior
First: Sam Wilson (Lotus 20/22)
Second: Jon Milicevic (Cooper T59)
Third: Andrew Hibberd (Brabham BT6)

Race 16: RAC Tourist Trophy for Historic pre-1963 GT
First: Oliver/Pearson (Ferrari 250GT Berlinetta SWB)
Second: Cottingham/Cottingham (Jaguar E-Type)
Third: Hunt/Blakeney-Edwards (AC Cobra)

Race 17: FIA Masters Historic Formula One
First: Martin Stretton (Tyrrell 012)
Second: Steve Hartley (Arrows A4)
Third: Christophe D'Ansembourg (Williams FW07/C)

Race 18: Group C Endurance
First: Bob Berridge (Mercedes C11)
Second: Justin Law – Jaguar XJR8)
Third: Steve Tandy (Nissan R90)

Race 19: Jet Super Touring Car Trophy
First: Rob Huff (Ford Mondeo)
Second: James Dodd (Honda Accord)
Third: Stewart Whyte (Honda Accord)

Race 20: Jack Brabham Memorial Trophy for HGPCA pre-1966 GP Cars
First: Jason Minshaw (Brabham BT4)
Second: Jon Farley (Brabham BT11)
Third: Miles Griffiths (Cooper T51)

Race 21: Maserati Centenary Trophy for HGPCA pre-1961 GP Cars
First: Philip Walker (Lotus 16)
Second: Julian Bronson (Scarab Offenhauser)
Third: Tony Wood (TecMec Maserati F415)

Race 22: Mustang Celebration Trophy
First: Leo Voyazides (Ford Falcon)
Second: Mike Gardiner (Ford Falcon)
Third: Tom Roche (Ford Mustang)

JET SUPER TOURING CAR TROPHY

James Dodd driving the Honda Accord clinched a win in the Saturday race and a second place on Sunday in 2014. The photo opposite is from the 2015 running of the Super Touring Car Trophy where Dodd brought the same car home second on Saturday; but did not start in Sunday's race.

SILVERSTONE CLASSIC 2014

July 25th. – July 27th.

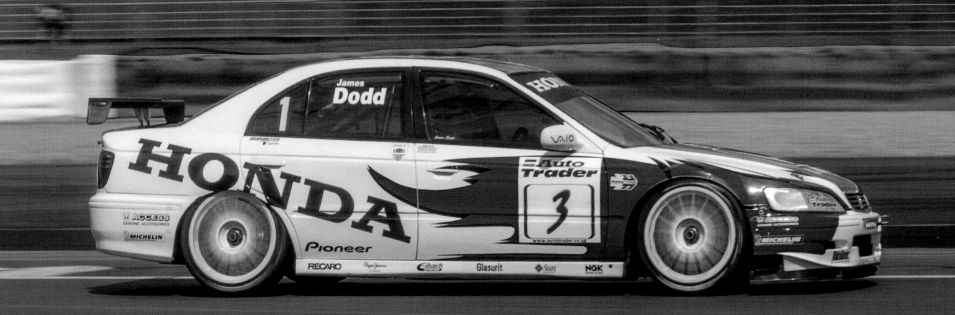

Ninth place finisher, the Lotus 15 of Dion Kremer (#70), about to be passed by the second placed Lister Knobbly (#5) of Gary Pearson through Abbey curve in the Stirling Moss Trophy race for pre-1961 Sports Cars.

Silverstone celebrated 25 years of their vast Classic weekend in late July. Although blighted by traditional British summer weather on Friday and Sunday, a record crowd turned up on sunny Saturday.

They boosted total three-day weekend attendance to more than 100,000 at the Jet-backed anniversary. Star attractions supported a 20-race bill, including major rock n'roll acts, headlined by *Status Quo*.

We particularly enjoyed Saturday's under 2-litre touring car event and, also on the Saturday, the Masters Historic Formula 1, along with the Stirling Moss Trophy for Pre-'61 sports cars, won by the glorious Gregor Fisken Ferrari 246S, beating off two Listers on the way.

Dry conditions allowed the largest ever Masters F1 pack full speed ahead and the colourful sight of a banana yellow Fittipaldi F5A showing non-period speed as it headed the pack, until pole-position man Martin Stretton fought his way to the front, with another Tyrrell finishing third.

Plenty of chassis variety in the F1 field (most pre-1982) included various Lotus types in the emotive black and gold Players livery, Arrows, Williams of varied eras. Just one McLaren and a single Ligier appeared.

Also adding to a premium race spectator experience, a boxy Surtees, Shadow and a 6-wheeler March.

Rarities continued with a brace of LECs, Hesketh, Penske and a Spirit (a 1984 pioneer for Honda power).

A single but correctly liveried Brabham BT33 was the oldest design entered (1971), but raced well in midfield for America's Duncan Dayton.

The sub-2-litre tourers had been headed by a Mini Cooper S on wet Friday qualifying; but on Saturday the Lotus Cortina mob headed for the front, interrupted only by Jackie Oliver's Laranca BMW 1800 TiSA and the Banks boys in the family Alfaholics Alfa Romeo Giulia Sprint GTA.

The Minis staged the best close racing longest as they fell down the order, but the Honda BTCC duo of Matt Neal/Gordon 'Flash' Shedden used their track craft to the max and held the Saturday lead at the finish after weaving through much of the large grid.

The final Saturday order was a Lotus Cortina 1-2-3, but the Oliver/Shaw shared BMW was fifth after holding second during the initial laps.

There was so much more to see we cannot report all the other races, but we list the race results on a later page.

Over 1,500 privately owned cars participated in track parades and the motor clubs once again turned out in force, so that you could browse from Alfa and AC through Caterhams (including a live action drift track on the infield) to Zagato-bodied exotica.

Yes, there were Ferraris by the score—mostly recent rather than the multi-million classic V12s—but also Astons, Maseratis and Lamborghinis if you have Italian tastes.

We travelled to and from Silverstone in the fromthedrivingseat.com project Lotus Elise and thus admired strong displays from at least three Lotus clubs, including the low drag original Elite representatives.

On the classic front there was the inevitable Silverstone Auctions collection, but there was nothing inevitable about the ex-Gordon Spice Motorcraft red BTCC class-winning Capri 3-litre realising over £90,000!

The flying displays are particularly appropriate at this ex-airfield track, and Saturday's menu catered for by the Battle of Britain Memorial Flight with their 'clipped' wing (low altitude) Spitfire Mk. LF XVIE rather than the traditional elliptically winged Supermarine machine.

We were lucky to attend on the only dry day, but the Silverstone Classic is now so established as a family-friendly event that it can keep the crowds coming even when the English summer does its worst.

JDW

FIA MASTERS HISTORIC FORMULA ONE

Jamie Constable (1977 Shadow DN8) leads Duncan Dayton (1971 Brabham BT33) around Copse corner during the Saturday running of the Historic F1 race.

STIRLING MOSS TROPHY

A sparkling drive in the Saturday sunshine saw Gregor Fisken take this glorious Ferrari 246S to victory over the second and third placed Lister Knobblies of Gary Pearson and Tony Wood/Will Nuthall in the Stirling Moss Trophy for pre-1961 Sports Cars .

With styling similar to the 250 Testa Rossa; but with a 2.4 litre V6 engine derived from that used in Ferrari's F1 cars, the 246S' first competition outing was in the 1960 Buenos Aires 100km in the hands of Ludovico Scarfiotti and José Froilán González; but the pair did not finish. Scarfiotti scored fourth in that year's Targa Florio sharing a 246S with Willy Mairesse. Another 246S driven by Wolfgang von Trips and Phil Hill came second in the same race, behind the Porsche 718 of Jo Bonnier and Hans Hermann.

STIRLING MOSS TROPHY

Sixteen of the 48 Lister Knobblies built by Brian Lister's company were powered by Chevrolet V8 engines and this is probably the most famous. Still wearing its Dean Van Lines sponsorship livery from when it campaigned in the USA between 1958 and 1960,

The car is driven here by owner Roberto Giordanelli who took the car to a respectable eleventh place in the Stirling Moss Trophy race.

STIRLING MOSS TROPHY

The Cottingham/Twyman Tojiero Jaguar qualified 15th on the grid for the Stirling Moss Trophy and advanced to sixth at the chequered flag.

David Murray of Ecurie Ecosse commissioned John Tojiero to build him a car for the 1959 Le Mans 24 Hours using a smaller capacity Jaguar engine to conform to the new 3-litre limit for the World Sports Car Championship. Driven by Ron Flockhart and Jock Lawrence the car was running well and up to fourth place when the head gasket went after 11 hours. The car struggled on until the engine eventually seized in the small hours of Sunday morning.

The car was later fitted with a taller block 3.8 litre Jaguar engine (hence the power bulge in the bonnet) and competed in the RAC Tourist Trophy at Goodwood the same year driven by Masten Gregory and Jim Clark. The pair had the car up to seventh when Gregory went straight on at Woodcote, burying the car in the earth bank and suffering a broken collarbone after being thrown (or jumping) from the car.

WARWICK BANKS TROPHY

BTCC duo of Matt Neal and Gordon Shedden in #152 led Lotus Cortinas to the first four places at the flag in the Warwick Banks Trophy for under 2-litre Touring Cars, after beating off the challenge of pole-sitting Mini Coopers, hard-charging BMWs and Alfas.

WARWICK BANKS TROPHY

Jackie Oliver/Richard Shaw piloted the Laranca BMW 1800 TiSA (#100) to a strong fifth place behind the Lotus Cortinas. The Banks brothers in the Alfaholics Alfa Romeo Giulia Sprint GTA (#89) were quick while they lasted but unfortunately retired on lap 13.

BMW marketed the 1800 Ti as the car you could win races in at the weekend and drive to work in on Monday.

FIA MASTERS HISTORIC FORMULA ONE

Two on this spread from the lesser known manufacturers of Formula One cars.

The car above is a LEC CRP1. David Purley's father Charlie had made his fortune from his LEC Refrigeration business and after David won the 1976 British F5000 championship in a Mike Pilbeam modified Chevron B30 Charlie asked Pilbeam to design a car for LEC Refrigeration Racing in which to contest the 1977 F1 season.

The CRP1 made its first appearance at the Race of Champions at Brands Hatch in March 1977 where David drove it into sixth place. At a rain-disrupted race in Belgium David briefly got the CRP1 up to third before having to pit for a tyre change; but during pre-qualifying at the British GP the throttle stuck open on the car and he crashed into the sleepers at Becketts with tremendous force suffering multiple fractures. A second CRP1 was built and after his recovery David drove that in minor race series, but he never drove in F1 again. WDK Motorsport built a new CRP1 in 2014, and both cars were in this race at Silverstone in 2015.

An ex-paratrooper, David Purley was awarded the George Medal for his heroic attempts to save Roger Williamson when his car crashed at the 1973 Dutch GP. After retiring from motor racing Purley turned to competition aerobatics. He died in July 1985 when his Pitts Special plane crashed into the sea off Bognor Regis.

FIA MASTERS HISTORIC FORMULA ONE

Here's another rarity, the Theodore TR1 seen here with Phillip Hall at the wheel during the FIA Masters Historic F1 race on Saturday, when he finished in 20th spot; but did not finish in Sunday's running.

Hong Kong millionaire Theodore 'Teddy' Yip commissioned Ron Tauranac to design and build two F1 cars for his Theodore Racing team to contest the 1978 season. The TR1 was not a success, with Eddie Cheever failing to qualify for the first two races of the season, while Keke Rosberg wrote one car off in practice for the South African GP; but started in the second car only to retire on lap 15 with clutch problems. This was to be the TR1's only F1 championship start, although Rosberg gave the TR1 its sole F1 victory at the non-championship International Trophy at Silverstone that same year, when he overcame torrential rain while many big names spun off in the dreadful conditions.

After failing to qualify at four more championship GPs Theodore Racing abandoned the TR1 mid-season, replacing it with a Wolf WR3.

Rob Hall qualified this Ligier JS/17 from 1981 on the third row of the grid for Saturday's Historic F1 race; but completed just five laps before retiring.

Powered by a Talbot-badged Matra V12 engine the JS/17 first appeared with conventional suspension which was replaced with a hydro-pneumatic system later in the year. Drivers in 1981 were Jacques Lafitte, Jean-Pierre Jabouille, Jean-Pierre Jarier and Patrick Tambay, with Lafitte taking wins in Austria and Canada to secure fourth place in the driver's championship.

Lafitte's points were sufficient to give the Ligier team fourth place in the Constructor's title as none of his other teammates scored any points.

FIA MASTERS HISTORIC FORMULA ONE

This 1982 Arrows A5 was driven by Neil Glover in both of the Historic F1 races at the 2015 Classic.

The single A5 appeared for the last three races of 1982 and was essentially a development car for the improved A6 which replaced it for the following year. Driven by Marc Surer for two of those races, at Dijon and Caeser's Palace, where Surer recorded the car's best finish in seventh place. Mauro Baldi drove the car for the Italian GP at Monza where he finished 12th and last.

The car was converted to A6 specification for the 1983 season, but later restored to A5 configuration for historic racing.

SUPER TOURING CAR TROPHY

Frank Wrathall took this Audi 80 quattro to a four second win over the Honda Accord of James Dodd in Saturday's Super Touring Car Trophy race.

This car competed in the Championnat de France de Supertourisme (French Super Touring Car Championship) between 1989 and 1993 winning the title in 1991 driven by Xavier Lapeyre, with Frank Biela repeating the feat in 1993. In 1991 Marc Soud took the title in another Audi 80 quattro.

SUPER TOURING CAR TROPHY

A mix of manufacturers. From left: #98 Vauxhall Vectra driven by John Cleland; #123 Ford Capri driven by Ric Wood; #29 Honda Accord driven by Alex Schooledge and Paul Rivett; #84 BMW E30 M3 driven by Tom Houlbrook.

The Honda Accord, chassis HR011, has a varied history. Having raced at the 1993 Spa 24 Hours, driven by Richard Piper, Philip Verellen and Vincent Vosse, where it was eliminated with suspension damage after an accident, the car spent many years racing in the UK and Norway before being purchased by Schooledge in 2014.

Race 1: **Peter Arundell Trophy for Historic Formula Junior**
First: Sam Wilson (Lotus 20/22)
Second: Jonathan Hughes (Brabham BT6)
Third: Callum Grant (Merlyn Mk5/7)

Race 2: **Stirling Moss Trophy for Pre '61 Sports Cars**
First: Gregor Fisken (Ferrari 246S)
Second: Garry Pearsont (Lister Jaguar Knobbly)
Third: Wood/Nuthall (Lister Knobbly)

Race 3: **Warwick Banks Trophy for Under 2-litre Touring Cars**
First: Neal/Shedden (Ford Lotus Cortina)
Second: Sumpter/Jordan (Ford Lotus Cortina)
Third: Meaden/Tromans (Ford Lotus Cortina)

Race 4: **Kidston Trophy for Pre War Sports Cars**
First: Wakeman/Blakeney-Edwards
(Frazer Nash Super Sports)
Second: Gareth Burnett (Talbot 105 Alpine)
Third: Rüdiger Friedrichs (Alvis Speed 20 SA)

Race 5: **FIA Masters Historic Formula One**
First: Martin Stretton (Tyrrell 12)
Second: Sam Hancock (Fittipaldi F5A)
Third: Loic Deman (Tyrrell 10)

Race 6: **Super Touring Car Trophy**
First: Frank Wrathall (Audi 80 quattro)
Second: James Dodd (Honda Accord)
Third: Stewart Whyte (Honda Accord)

Race 7: **Maserati Trophy for HGPCA Pre '66 GP Cars**
First: Tim Harvey (Cooper T51)
Second: Will Nuthall (Cooper T53)
Third: Jon Fairley (Brabham BT11)

Race 8: **Jet Battle of Britain Trophy**
First: Mike Whitaker (TVR Griffith)
Second: Matt Nicoll-Jones (Jaguar E-Typ)e
Third: Steve Soper (Jaguar E-Type)

Race 9: **FIA Masters Historic Sports Cars**
First: Martin O'Connell (Chevron B19)
Second: Franchitti/Meaden (Lola T70 Mk3B)
Third: Tromans/Stretton (Lola T70 Mk3B)

Race 10: **International Trophy for Classic GT Cars (Pre '66)**
First: Martin O'Connell (Jaguar E-Type)
Second: Gans/Wolfe (AC Cobra)
Third: Mike Whitaker (TVR Griffith)

Race 11: **Group C**
First: Christophe D'Ansembourg (Jaguar XJR14)
Second: Bob Berridge (Nissan R90)
Third: Steve Tandy (Spice SE90)

Race 12: **RAC Woodcote Trophy for Pre-1956 Sports Cars**
First: Young/Ward (Jaguar C-Type)
Second: Gary Pearson (Jaguar D-Type)
Third: Friedrichs/Hadfield (Aston Martin DB3S)

Race 13: **Peter Arundell Trophy for Historic Formula Junior**
First: Sam Wilson (Lotus 20/22)
Second: Jonathan Hughes (Brabham BT6)
Third: Callum Grant (Merlyn Mk5/7)

Race 14: **RAC Tourist Trophy for Historic Cars (Pre-1963 GT)**
First: Freidrichs/Hadfield (Aston Martin DB4 GT)
Second: Melling/Hall (Jaguar E-Type)
Third: Cottingham/Cottingham (Jaguar E-Type)

Race 15: **FIA Masters Historic Formula One**
First: Martin Stretton (Tyrrell 012)
Second: Sam Hancock (Fittipaldi F5A)
Third: Andy Wolfe (Tyrrell 011)

Race 16: **HSCC Guards Trophy**
First: Watson/O'Connell (Chevron B)8
Second: Dion Kremer (Elva Mk8)
Third: Hadfield/Schryver (Chevron B6)

Race 17: **Super Touring Car Trophy**
First: Stewart Whyte (Honda Accord)
Second: Patrick Watts (Peugeot 406)
Third: Jan Bot (BMW E30 M3)

Race 18: **Group C**
First: Steve Tandy (Spice SE90)
Second: David Methley (Spice SE89)
Third: Aaron Scott (Spice SE86)

Race 19: **Maserati Trophy for HGPCA Pre '66 GP Cars**
First: Tim Harvey (Cooper T51)
Second: Julian Bronson (Scarab Offenhause)r
Third: Will Nuthall (Cooper T53)

Race 20: **Jet Battle of Britain Trophy**
First: Matt Nicoll-Jones (Jaguar E-Type)
Second: Mike Whitaker (TVR Griffith)
Third: Jonathan Lewis (Austin Mini Cooper S)

MID-FIELD RUNNERS IN RACE 5: FIA MASTERS HISTORIC FORMULA ONE

#47 (Jeremy Smith, 1976 March 2-4-0 (finished in 21st place)

#6 (Max Smith-Hilliard, 1981 Williams FW07C (finished 10th)

#12 (Dan Collins, 1982 Lotus 91 (finished in 15th);

#28 (Chris Drake, 1976 Penske PC3 (DNF)

#30 (David Abbott,1982 Arrows A4 (finished in 24th)

Driving into the gathering twilight in the penultimate race on Saturday (International Trophy for pre-1966 Classic GT Cars), the Daniel and Dominique Reinhardt Jaguar E- Type leads the Lotus Elan of Urs and Arlette Müller, the Leo Voyazides and Simon Hadfield Shelby Daytona Cobra, followed by an MGB carrying the race number 86, which according to the official race card is a Tojeiro EE-Buick driven by Till Becholtsheimer!

SILVERSTONE CLASSIC 2016

July 29th. – July 31st.

In its 26th year the Silverstone Classic was bigger than ever with a packed programme of 20 races over the weekend, plus demonstration sessions for Legends of Modern F1, 90s Endurance legends, and World GP Bike Legends (although some of these continued for too long. If they're not racing, then 20 minutes of cars just circulating can become a bit of a yawn-fest.

Still, plenty of excitement in a varied series of races that included everything from Historic Formula Junior to thundering Can-Am cars by way of Historic F1 and Group C cars.

Our special interest was 'Tin-Top' Sunday with four races for saloons. These included exciting wheel-to-wheel (panel-to-panel?) action in the John Fitzpatrick Trophy race (as can be seen in these photos.

Off-track interest continued with manufacturer displays (Porsche standing out with a simply enormous presence, plus what seemed like thousands of owners' cars.

75 car clubs were exhibiting on the infield, with 30 of them having parade laps. That was probably too many to be honest, as at times the circuit looked more like the M25 in rush hour. However those who took part seemed to have enjoyed themselves.

There were plenty of opportunities to get up close and personal to cars and drivers in both the National and International paddocks.

Additionally, numerous sideshows kept families happy (plus *The Boomtown Rats* and *The Stranglers* performing on Friday and Saturday nights. The versatile Silverstone Classic has become a must-do event for petrolheads.

Those with more than a few quid burning a hole in their pockets could get rid of it at the Silverstone Auctions. They had some tempting competition and classic cars for sale, alongside loads of motoring memorabilia.

Meanwhile James Hunt fans were rewarded with a commemorative display of his cars in the International Pits and the presence of son Freddie Hunt.

Murray Walker with Freddie Hunt at the wheel of his father's F1 McLaren at the 2016 Silverstone Classic Media Preview day.

The Avill/Hyett (#69) and O'Brien/Davison (#40) Lotus Cortinas indulge in a spot of panel beating during the John Fitzpatrick Trophy race for under 2 litre Touring Cars.

70

FORD LOTUS CORTINA

Colin Chapman got Harry Munday to design a twin-cam version of the Ford 4-cylinder engines at varying cubic capacities. The Lotus-Ford Twin Cam made its first appearance at 1498cc in a Lotus 23 driven by Jim Clark at the Nürburgring in 1962. Ford's Walter Hayes asked Chapman to fit the newly developed twin-cam engine to 1,000 Cortinas in order to homologate the car for Group 2 Touring Car racing, when capacity could be increased to 1558cc for production Elan and Lotus Cortina, or just under the 1600cc international racing limit in competition trim..

The Lotus Cortina used an updated version of the 1499cc twin-cam motor that earlier appeared in Lotus 23, enlarged to 1558cc for Lotus Cortina production and using the entire bottom end of the 5-bearing 1599cc Ford 116E crossflow motor. This led to some compromises versus the unit used in Lotus 23 as flat top pistons were needed for production Lotus Cortina, which led to some combustion chamber changes. Race tuning for the Ford-backed Team Lotus cars was entrusted to either Cosworth or BRM.

Two-door Cortina bodyshells were shipped to Lotus in Cheshunt where the 1558cc twin-cam engines and close-ratio gearbox were installed along with extensive suspension changes including a radical rear set-up which swapped the leaf springs for coil springs, dampers and an unreliable 'A' bracket from floorpan to diff casing, although this was changed back to the more reliable leaf springs on production cars from mid-1965.

Lightweight aluminium panels were used on the doors, bonnet, and boot for the homologation build; but not for later road cars, and all the cars were finished in white with a green stripe (although one superstitious customer thought green an unlucky colour and requested a dark blue stripe).

A Lotus Cortina with a front wheel waving in the air was a common sight in 1964 when Jim Clark ran out an easy winner of the British Saloon Car Championship. Meanwhile Alan Mann Racing entered Lotus Cortinas in the European Touring Car Challenge with good results, including a 1-2 finish at Brands Hatch for the pairings of John Whitmore/Peter Procter and Henry Taylor/Peter Harper.

Also in 1964, in the USA, Lotus Cortinas driven by Jackie Stewart/Mike Beckwith and John Whitmore/Tony Hegbourne finished in first and second spots in the 12 Hour race at Marlboro Park Speedway in Maryland.

In 1965 Lotus Cortinas were regular winners in saloon car racing, including winning the European Touring Car Championship for Alan Mann Racing in the hands of Sir John Whitmore. Jacky Ickx took the Belgian Touring Car championship with an end of season win at Zolder, also in an Alan Mann Racing Lotus Cortina.

Lotus Cortinas featured in rallying as well, with the first works victory coming in 1965 when Roger Clark and Graham Robson won the Welsh International rally, although the cars were only durable for rallying with the conventional leaf sprung rear end as the Chapman coils and A bracket set up resulted in major oil leaks from the diff.

PJO

JOHN FITZPATRICK TROPHY

Andy Wolfe stormed away from pole in this 1965 Ford Lotus Cortina to take a five second lead at the end of lap one of the John Fitzpatrick Trophy for Under 2 Litre Touring Cars. He dominated the race before handing over to Richard Meaden who came home ahead of the Neil Brown/Richard Dutton Lotus Cortina by a 20 second margin.

2016

JOHN FITZPATRICK TROPHY

Ford loaned a number of the newly homologated Twin Cam Escorts to Alan Mann Racing to contest the 1968 British Saloon Car Championship, which Frank Gardner won using Escort XOO 349F and a redeveloped Cortina Lotus pioneering a prototype rack and pinion steering system: both featured Lotus-Ford Twin Cam power..

Jackie Oliver was an occasional driver of XOO 347F during the 1968 season, once beating Frank Gardner at Brands Hatch.

XOO 347F is driven here at the 2016 Silverstone Classic by Alan Mann's son Henry.

MASERATI TROPHY

Opposite lock and right front wheel high in the air, Rod Jolley powers the 1958 Cooper T45/51 through Copse during the Maserati Trophy race for pre 1966 GP cars.

The Cooper Car Company has a special place in F1 history as a Cooper was the first rear-engined car to score a Formula One victory when Stirling Moss drove a Rob Walker entered Cooper T43 to win the 1958 Argentine GP.

In 1959 Jack Brabham became the first F1 World Champion driving a car with the engine behind him when he won that year's championship in a Cooper T51.

MASERATI TROPHY

Winner of the Maserati Trophy race was Will Nuthall in this Cooper T53 from 1960. After enjoying a race-long tussle with Jon Fairley in the 1964 Brabham BT11/19, during which they swapped the lead a few times, Nuthall sneaked past on the last lap to claim the win.

RAC WOODCOTE TROPHY FOR PRE-1956 SPORTS CARS

BTCC ace John Cleland at the wheel of his shiny, bare-metal finish 1955 Lotus Mark 6.

Lotus Cars first production model, the Mark 6 was available from 1952 to 1955. Purchased in kit form, the Mark 6 could be fitted with a variety of engines enabling it to be competitive in a number of events. In their first competition appearance at Silverstone in July 1952 Mark 6s scored two second place finishes, and in the hands of Colin Chapman, Peter Gammon and Mike Anthony dominated club racing before production ceased.

John Cleland was successful in the British Thunder Saloon Car Championship in the 1980s driving the Peter Brock 1984 Bathurst 1000 winning Holden VK Commodore, which his father had purchased from the Brock team, winning the championship title in 1986 and 1988.

Moving to the British Touring Car Championship in 1989 he won that title in his first year driving a Vauxhall Astra GTE. Between 1990 and 1995, at the wheel of a Vauxhall Cavalier, Cleland finished in the top five of the BTCC every year and he took the title again in 1995. Cleland had 208 races with 98 podium finishes over a ten year career in BTCC (1989-1999).

He also raced in the Bathurst 100 at the Mount Panorama circuit in Australia with his best finish in 2001 taking second place in a Ford Falcon co-driven with Brad Jones.

2016

RAC WOODCOTE TROPHY FOR PRE-1956 SPORTS CARS

1953 Cooper Bristol T25 driven by Malcolm Harrison and Patrick Watts.

Bristol's 2 litre engine as used in this Cooper, and many other sports cars of the period, was based on the BMW engine used in the BMW 328, the rights for which Bristol acquired after the Second World War and which powered all Bristol cars until the advent of the Chrysler V8 powered models in the 1960s.

Cooper T25s were successfully raced in period by many well-known drivers including Tony Crook (later owner of Bristol Cars), John Coombs and Tommy Sopwith. In 1958 Sopwith tied on points with Jack Sears in the British Saloon Car Championship, the title being awarded to Sears after a 'shoot-out' between the two in identical Riley One Point Fives at Brands Hatch.

HISTORIC TOURING CAR CHALLENGE

Paul Pochciol and James Hanson shared driving duties and qualified this thunderous 1977 Broadspeed Jaguar XJ12 on fourth spot on the grid; but did not appear for the race.

Jaguar's Broadspeed-prepared XJ12 Coupé made its race debut in the 1976 Tourist Trophy race at Silverstone where Derek Bell excited the crowd by putting the new car on pole almost two seconds faster than the Luigi BMW CSL of Pierre Dieudonne. During the first laps Bell fought with Gunnar Nilsson in the second Luigi BMW until a blown tyre forced him to pit. Five laps later he rejoined and fought his way back into contention setting a new Group 2 lap record in the process.

The damage caused by the earlier tyre incident however resulted in a broken drive shaft and loss of a rear wheel after David Hobbs had taken over and the car was parked off the Hangar Straight.

In 1977 Jaguar announced a two-car team of XJ12Cs with driver pairings of Derek Bell/Andy Rouse and John Fitzpatrick/Tim Schenken. A positive start to the season saw the Jaguars on pole for the first two races at Monza and Salzburgring; but both cars did not finish. That set the pattern for the rest of the year (pole position but DNF) only broken by a second place at the Nürburgring and a fourth at Silverstone.

After pouring money into the project, and with no wins to show for it, Leyland Cars decided to pull the plug at the end of that year after only 18 months. With six pole positions from just eight races the big cats showed great promise and with further development could have had a really successful 1978 season.

HISTORIC TOURING CAR CHALLENGE

Jagermeister-liveried 1975 BMW 3.0 CSL, driven by Peter Mullen and Patrick Blakeney-Edwards, pursued by the Clark/Wills piloted 1979 Chevrolet Camaro. Pictured in Friday qualifying, the BMW unfortunately expired on the first lap of the race.

HISTORIC TOURING CAR CHALLENGE

Alfa Romeo's Alfetta GTV6 enjoyed considerable success in the early 1980s, winning the European Touring Car Championship in an unprecedented consecutive four years from 1982-1985. Andy Rouse won the 1983 British Saloon Car Championship also driving an Alfetta GTV6 sponsored by Industrial Control Services.

Lella Lombardi, the only female driver to have competed and scored points in Formula One, campaigned the Jolly Club GTV6 in the ETCC.

Paul Clayson was behind the wheel at the Silverstone Classic.

HISTORIC TOURING CAR CHALLENGE

The Trans-American sedan (saloon car) Championship was inaugurated in 1966 with the first round at Sebring where Jochen Rindt took the win driving an Alfa Romeo GTA.

For the 1970 series Penske Racing prepared and entered American Motors (AMC) Javelin's driven by Mark Donohue and Peter Revson. Donohue won three out of the eleven race series and the AMC cars just missed out on the title to Ford; but Donohue's seven wins the following year secured the 1971 championship for AMC.

In the UK David Howes, the AMC and Jeep distributor for the UK, built this Javelin to Group 2 regulations and drove it in the 1972 and 1973 British Saloon Car Championship before the car was put into dry storage in 1975.

Marc Devis bought the untouched car from David Howes and, with only minor refurbishment and safety updates, was out behind the wheel at Silverstone.

HISTORIC TOURING CAR CHALLENGE

Team Butch Broadspeed entered four Triumph Dolomite Sprints in the 1974 Spa 24 Hours, carrying race numbers 45, 46, 47, and 48. Two of these were still running at the end of 24 hours with the number 48 car driven by Andy Rouse and Tony Dron taking the fifth place overall, and the number 45 car of John Hine and Freddy Grainal in ninth.

Car number 47 driven by Julien Vernaeve and John Handley retired after twelve hours, while Claude De Wael and Etienne Stalpaert in the number 46 car almost made it to the finish before a suspension failure sidelined them with an hour or so to go.

This Dolomite was driven at Silverstone by Sarah Bennett-Baggs and Andrew Frankel.

HISTORIC TOURING CAR CHALLENGE

Bastos-liveried Chevrolet Camaro Z28 driven by Claude Bourgoigne, Reine Wisell and John Cooper took pole position for the 24 hour race at Spa-Francorchamps in 1981. Leading from the start for the first hour, a detached cooling fan blade resulted in a half hour stop to replace fan and alternator.

Although the Camaro returned to the fray and ran reliably through the night, the September 1981 issue of *Motor Sport* magazine reported that it retired on the Sunday morning with either a "starter motor" or "head gasket" failure.

Owner David Clark drove this Camaro at Silverstone, although the car only lasted five laps before retiring.

FIA MASTERS HISTORIC FORMULA ONE

Nick Padmore drove this 1981 Williams FW07C to first place in both Saturday's and Sunday's running of the Historic F1 race.

The Patrick Head designed FW07 gave Williams their first race win when Clay Regazzoni came home almost 25 seconds ahead of the field in the 1979 British GP at Silverstone. His teammate Alan Jones scored four more wins that season to place the Williams team second in the Constructor's Title.

In 1980 Carlos Reutemann replaced Regazzoni alongside Jones, both now driving the FW07B with which Jones won five of the eleven rounds to take the Drivers' Championship and secure the Constructor's Title for Williams, the first of nine for the team.

The FW07C variant appeared for the 1981 season, again with Jones and Reutemann driving for Williams. Reutemann challenged for the Driver's title missing out by one point to Nelson Piquet, with Jones a further three points behind in third place. Williams however secured the Constructor's Championship. If both cars hadn't suffered from a misfire caused by fuel surge in some races either Jones or Reutemann could have taken the Driver's Title as well.

FIA MASTERS HISTORIC FORMULA ONE

Second place in both of the weekend's Historic F1 race was taken by Belgian Loic Deman in the Tyrrell 010 from 1980.

With sponsorship backing from the Italian domestic appliance manufacturer Candy, Tyrrell entered the 1980 F1 season using the 009 car from the previous year until the new Maurice Phillipe designed 010 appeared for the third race in South Africa where Jean-Pierre Jarier finished seventh and the other car driven by Derek Daly retired with a puncture.

Daly's two fourth place finishes and Jarier's three fifth places secured them 12th and 13th in the Driver's Championship, while Candy Team Tyrrell finished in sixth position in the Constructor's Championship.

2016

American driver Doug Mockett at the wheel of the Penske PC3.

After multiple successes in Can-Am and Trans-Am with Sunoco-sponsored cars driven by Mark Donohue, Roger Penske turned his attention to Formula One and set up shop in Poole, Dorset UK to build his own F1 car, the Penske PC1 designed by ex-Brabham engineer Geoff Ferris, and driven by Donohue.

The PC1 was not that successful, with Donohue's best finish being fifth at the 1975 Swedish GP, and for the British GP the PC1 was replaced with a March 751. Donohue crashed heavily during warm-up for the Austrian GP and, although seemingly uninjured, he died two days later from a brain haemorrhage.

In 1976, driving the new PC3 and later PC4 John Watson finished third in the French and British GPs and scored Penske Racing's first, and only, F1 win in Austria. Watson finished the 1975 season in seventh place in the driver's championship with the Penske team taking fifth place in the constructor's title. But with sponsorship hard to find Penske withdrew from Formula One at the end of 1975 to concentrate on Indycars and NASCAR.

FIA MASTERS HISTORIC FORMULA ONE

There's a link between this car and the one on the facing page, as the ATS HS1 (driven at the Silverstone Classic by Christian Perrier) is basically a Penske PC4 initially updated by Robin Heard after ATS bought their FOCA membership from March.

Driven by Jochen Mass and Jean-Pierre Jarier in the 1978 F1 season the cars were not successful, with Jarier's eighth place finish in South Africa being their best result of the season.

After Jarier left he was replaced by Keke Rosberg who had no more luck with the HS1, nor with the replacement D1 car which he drove in the last two races of 1978, the US GP in which a gearbox failure forced retirement and the Canadian GP where he finished but was not classified.

FIA MASTERS HISTORIC FORMULA ONE

1975 Maki F101 driven at the 2016 Silverstone Classic by Marc Devis.

After Honda withdrew from F1 in 1968, it would be another six years until a Japanese constructor graced F1 paddocks. The small Maki team founded by Kenji Mimura first appeared at Brands Hatch for the 1974 British GP with the Maki F101 powered by the Ford Cosworth DFV V8. Driven by New Zealander Howden Ganley, the car failed to qualify at Brands, then during qualifying for the following German GP a rear suspension failure caused Ganley to crash badly in practice suffering serious ankle injuries that ended his F1 career.

The car was shipped back to Japan for repair and did not appear again until the 1975 Dutch GP at Zandvoort with Hiroshi Fushida, the first Japanese driver to enter an F1 race (and also the first Japanese driver to race at Le Mans) at the wheel. The engine blew and, as the team had no spare, he did not start. Fushida was replaced by Tony Trimmer for the German GP but he did not qualify, nor did he qualify for the Austrian GP.

Maki made their only F1 start at the non-championship 1975 Swiss Grand Prix held at Dijon-Prenois in France, where Trimmer came 13th and last, nine laps down on Clay Regazzoni's winning Ferrari.

The team only appeared once more after that at the 1976 season finisher, the Japanese GP, with an upgraded version of the car (the F102A) again driven by Trimmer. Unsurprisingly they failed to qualify and disappeared for good.

FIA MASTER HISTORIC FORMULA ONE

Martin Stretton drove this 1983 Tyrrell 012 to sixth place in Sunday's race, after finishing towards the rear of the field on Saturday.

The Cosworth DFV powered Tyrrell 012 appeared for the 1983 season when turbocharged engines had arrived, and designer Maurice Phillipe had to make the car as light as possible to try and offset the power advantage of the turbos.

With sponsorship from Italian clothing brand Benetton for 1983, the car made its race debut at the 1983 Dutch Grand Prix with American driver Danny Sullivan at the wheel. Sullivan's best GP result that year was fifth at Monaco, although he placed second at the non-championship Race of Champions at Brand Hatch.

Sullivan later went on to a successful career in CART, winning the legendary "spin and win" 1985 Indy 500 and the CART Championship in 1988 driving for Penske Racing. He also drove a Dauer 962 LM to third at the 1994 Le Mans sharing with Thierry Boutsen and Hans-Joachim Stuck.

Sullivan's teammate Michele Alboreto scored a win in a Tyrrell 012 at the 1983 Detroit Grand Prix, the last win for the Tyrrell team and the last of 155 victories for the Cosworth DFV.

JET SUPER TOURING CAR TROPHY

Craig Davies in the Brooklyn-liveried Ford RS500 (#15) leads the Volvo S40 driven by Jason Minshaw. Minshaw finished eighth in the Saturday race ahead of Davies in ninth. Sunday's running saw Minshaw take third spot at the flag while Davies finished in eighth place.

Ford RS Dealer, Brooklyn Ford, prepared the RS500 for Chris Hodgetts to drive in the 1988/89 British Touring Car Championship.

A decade later Sweden's Rickard Rydell won the 1998 BTCC driving the TWR-prepared Volvo S40.

JET SUPER TOURING CAR TROPHY

Guy Minshaw drove this Audi A4 to a solid mid-field finish in both of the weekend's Super touring Car races, despite a loose bonnet in Saturday's race.

#44 Audi was entered in the 1995 ADAC SuperTourenWagen Cup by AZK Team Schneider and driven by Hans-Joachim Stuck to fourth in the championship.

Stuck is the son of the great pre-war German ace Hans Stuck who drove the fearsome V16, rear-engined Auto Union to victories in the 1934 German, Swiss and Czech Grand Prix races as well as winning a number of hill-climbs to win the German Mountain Championship, a feat he repeated three times, the last in 1960 driving a tiny BMW 700 RS, a complete contrast to the monstrous 1930s Auto Unions.

CAN-AM 50 INTERSERIE CHALLENGE TROPHY

"Lowest, most radical Can-Am yet" is how *Road & Track* magazine described the Shadow Mk1 when it made its first appearance in 1969. Don Nichols of Shadow commissioned Trevor Harris to design a car that combined the smallest possible chassis with a big-block V8. Harris' design incorporated many unique features including 10" front wheels, and radiators mounted behind the rear wheels to create a car with 35% less frontal area than comparable Can-Am cars. It was certainly radical but, due to lack of both development time and aerodynamic knowledge, it lacked reliability and retired in all the races in which it competed due to overheating despite many, usually counter-productive, modifications.

Harm Lagaaij (former head of design at Porsche) purchased this Shadow Mk1 in 2009 and restored the car to its original specification, as tested by Parnelli Jones and George Fulmer at Riverside and Laguna Seca, while solving the reliability problems that plagued the car in period along the way. He drove the car at the Classic where he also collected the award for the Most Admired Race Car.

2016

CAN-AM 50 INTERSERIE CHALLENGE TROPHY

The antithesis of the Shadow the huge, thundering McLaren M8F with its 8.8 litre engine was driven to second place in both race 7 and race 20 by Andrew Newall.

The orange McLarens dominated the Can-Am Series (also known as "The Bruce and Denny Show") between 1967 and 1971 with Bruce McLaren and Denny Hulme taking two championship titles between them, while Peter Revson took the team's last Can-Am championship win in 1971.

CAN-AM 50 INTERSERIE CHALLENGE

American driver Rick Carlino in the GRD S72 (#111) leads Matt Manderson in the Fred Davies Special (#22) into Copse during the opening laps of Saturday's race. Carlino finished in 18th and Derek Jones drove the car to ninth in Sunday's race. Manderson DNF'd in both races.

Group Racing Developments (GRD) was founded by ex-Lotus engineers in 1972 and Roger Williamson won that year's F3 national championships driving a GRD 372. GRD also built cars for F2, Formula Atlantic and Sports 200 classes during a short lived period until being taken over by Van Dieman in 1975.

The Fred Davies Special is, as the name suggests, a one-off designed and built in 1961-62 by English engineer Fred Davies who had moved to California; but never raced by him and subsequently sold to, and raced by, various European owners.

Davies fitted his Special with a Chevrolet V8 mated to a Huffaker gearbox, in a lightweight tubular space-frame chassis clothed in aluminium bodywork.

CAN-AM 50 INTERSERIE CHALLENGE

Belgian driver Marc Devis took this TOJ SC303 to ninth in Saturday's race and finished in seventh spot the following day. Jonathan Loader's Chevron B19 in the background finished both races in 14th and 12th place respectively.

German Jörg Obermoser raced in touring cars and sports cars, before deciding to create his own cars which he named TOJ (for Team Obermoser Jörg) in 1974.

The first car, a 2-litre sports racer inspired by the GRD he had raced previously, was the TOJ SC204. The 3-litre SC304, powered by a Cosworth DFV followed in 1976 making its first appearance at the Dijon 500 Kilometres driven by Obermoser and Rolf Stommelen where it was fast but retired after 30 laps with suspension damage. Obermoser won one race in the 1976 German Interserie championship, followed by two more victories the following year.

SC303 was the TOJ team's new car for 1978, but was nowhere near as successful. One car was entered for that year's Le Mans 24 hour race driven by Obermoser with Guy Chasseuil and Hubert Striebig but blew the engine in qualifying and did not start.

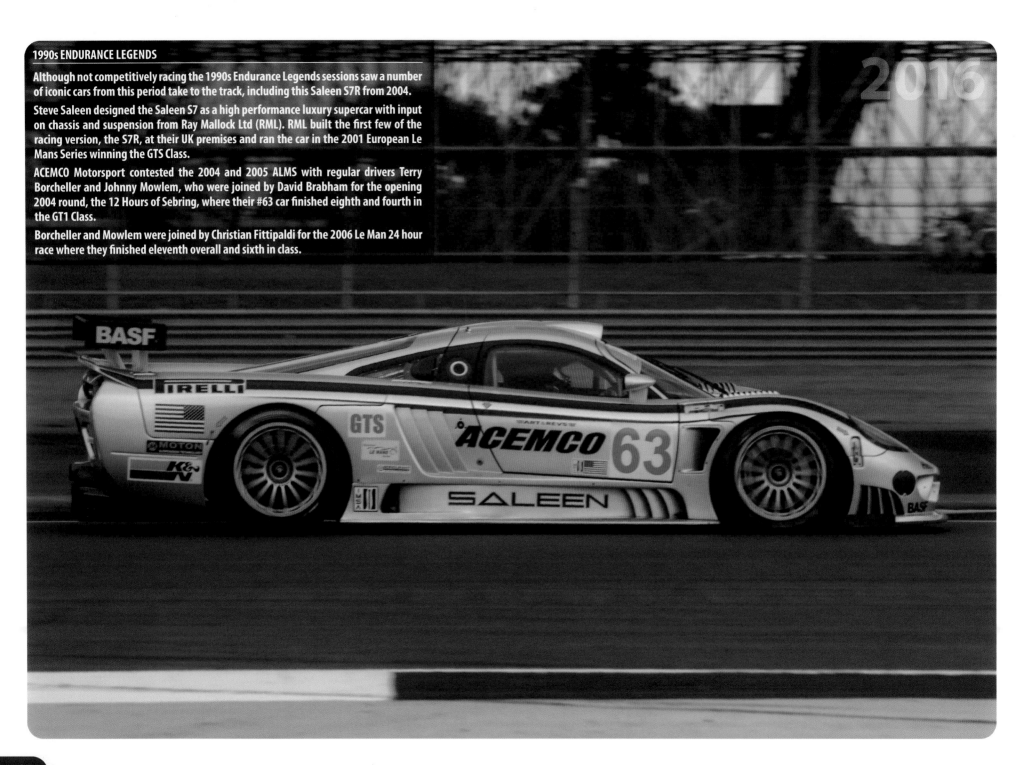

1990s ENDURANCE LEGENDS

Although not competitively racing the 1990s Endurance Legends sessions saw a number of iconic cars from this period take to the track, including this Saleen S7R from 2004.

Steve Saleen designed the Saleen S7 as a high performance luxury supercar with input on chassis and suspension from Ray Mallock Ltd (RML). RML built the first few of the racing version, the S7R, at their UK premises and ran the car in the 2001 European Le Mans Series winning the GTS Class.

ACEMCO Motorsport contested the 2004 and 2005 ALMS with regular drivers Terry Borcheller and Johnny Mowlem, who were joined by David Brabham for the opening 2004 round, the 12 Hours of Sebring, where their #63 car finished eighth and fourth in the GT1 Class.

Borcheller and Mowlem were joined by Christian Fittipaldi for the 2006 Le Man 24 hour race where they finished eleventh overall and sixth in class.

1990s ENDURANCE LEGENDS

Not really an Endurance Legend; but the Maserati Barchetta is an interesting oddity. The aluminium backbone chassis of the Barchetta carried a innovative three-piece carbon composite body and is powered by a 2-litre, twin-turbo V6 developing 350 bhp in a car weighing just 775kg.

Conceived by the then boss of Maserati, Alejandro de Tomaso, the *Grantrofeo Monomarco Barchetta Maserati* was a one-make race series aimed at amateur 'gentleman' drivers using these cars. The first year of the series in 1992 saw six races across Italy all of which were won easily by 1990 Le Mans winner Jon Neilsen (hardly the amateur driver for whom the series was intended).

Although the series expanded to eight Italian races, plus a race each in Holland and Denmark in 1999, the dominance of Neilsen and the paucity of entrants led to the series being cancelled at the end of that year with a total of just 16 cars having been built.

RACE RESULTS Silverstone Classic 2016

Race 1: **Commander Yorke Trophy for Historic Formula Junior**
First: Sam Wilson (Lotus 20/22)
Second: Andrew Hibberd (Lotus 22)
Third: Callum Grant (Merlyn Mk5/7)

Race 2: **Stirling Moss Trophy for Pre '61 Sports Cars**
First: Sam Hancock (Ferrari 246S)
Second: Richard Knight (Lister Costin Jaguar)
Third: Wood/Nuthall (Lister Knobbly)

Race 3: **RAC Tourist Trophy for Historic Cars (Pre'63 GT)**
First: Friedrichs/Hadfield (Aston Martin DB4GT)
Second: Hunt/Blakeny-Edwards (AC Cobra)
Third: Cottingham/Smith (Jaguar E-Type)

Race 4: **RAC Woodcote Trophy for Pre'56 Sports Cars**
First: Chris Ward (Cooper Jaguar T33)
Second: Wakeman/Blakeny-Edwards (Cooper T38)
Third: Wood/Wood (RGS Atlanta)

Race 5: **FIA Masters Historic Formula One**
First: Nick Padmore (Williams FW07)
Second: Loic Deman (Tyrrell 010)
Third: Gregory Thornton (Lotus 91/5)

Race 6: **JET Super Touring Car Trophy**
First: Colin Noble jnr. (Vauxhall Vectra)
Second: James Dodd (Honda Accord)
Third: Frank Wrathall (Audi A4)

Race 7: **Can-Am 50 Interserie Challenge**
First: Rob Hall (Matra MS670B/C)
Second: Andrew Newall (Mclaren M8F)
Third: John Grant (Mclaren M8C/D)

Race 8: **Maserati Trophy for HGPCA Pre '68 Grand Prix Cars**
First: Will Nuthall (Cooper T53)
Second: Jon Fairley (Brabham BT11)
Third: Peter Horsman (Lotus 18/21)

Race 9: **FIA Masters Historic Sports Cars**
First: Wills/Hall (Matra MS650)
Second: Oliver Bryant (Lola T70)
Third: Ward/Gibson (Lola T70)

Race 10: **International Trophy for Classic GT Cars (Pre '68)**
First: Voyazides/Hadfield (Shelby Daytona Cobra)
Second: Oliver Bryant (AC Cobra)
Third: Mike Whitaker (TVR Griffith)

Race 11: **Group C**
First: Nathan Kinch (Lola T92/10)
Second: Katsu Kubota (Nissan RC90K)
Third: Mark Sumpter (Porsche 962)

Race 12: **Commander Yorke Trophy for Historic Formula Junior**
First: Sam Wilson (Lotus 20/22)
Second: Andrew Hibberd (Lotus 22)
Third: Callum Grant (Merlyn Mk5/7)

Race 13: **John Fitzpatrick Trophy for Under 2 litre Touring Cars**
First: Wolfe/Meaden (Ford Lotus Cortina)
Second: Brown/Dutton (Ford Lotus Cortina)
Third: Banks/Banks (Alfa Romeo Giulia Sprint)

Race 14: **Historic Touring Car Challenge**
First: Whale/Whale (BMW M3 E30)
Second: Tromans/Meaden (Ford Capri)
Third: David Tomlin (Ford RS1800)

Race 15: **FIA Masters Historic Formula One**
First: Nick Padmore (Williams FW07)
Second: Loic Deman (Tyrrell 010)
Third: Ollie Hancock (Fittipaldi F5A0)

Race 16: **Big Engine Touring Cars (Pre '66)**
First: Craig Davies (Ford Mustang)
Second: Roger Wills (Mercury Comet Cyclone)
Third: Benjamin Beighton (Ford Mustang)

Race 17: **Group C**
First: Bob Berridge (Nissan R93)
Second: Mark Sumpter (Porsche 962)
Third: Katsu Kubota (Nissan RC90K)

Race 18: **JET Super Touring Car Trophy**
First: James Dodd (Honda Accord)
Second: Neil Smith (Alfa Romeo 156)
Third: Jason Minshaw (Volvo S40)

Race 19: **Maserati Trophy for HGPCA Pre '68 Grand Prix Cars**
First: Peter Horsman (Lotus 18/21)
Second: Rod Jolley (Cooper T45/51)
Third: Tony Wood (Maserati Tec Mec)

Race 20: **Can-Am 50 Interserie Challenge**
First: Rob Hall (Matra MS670B/C)
Second: Andrew Newall (Mclaren M8F)
Third: Michele Liguori (Lola T292)

CAN-AM 50 INTERSERIE CHALLENGE

Rob Hall took the 1974 Matra Simca MS670B/C to victory in both Can-Am 50 Interserie Challenge Trophy races over the 2016 Classic weekend. Here followed by the Lola T210 of Nick Pink and Scott Mansell.

The MS670 was introduced in 1972 when Matra entered three (and one MS660) for that year's Le Mans 24 Hour race. Driven by François Cevert/Howden Ganley, Henri Pescarolo/Graham Hill and Jean-Pierre Jabouille/David Hobbs, with the Pescarolo/Hill pairing winning the race by one lap from Cevert/Ganley.

That was the only appearance for the MS670 in 1972; but in 1973 and 1974 the MS670 B and C variants took Matra to two consecutive World Championship for Makes titles. Matra pulled out of motor racing at the end of that year.

Yellow flag at Abbey during the Kidston Trophy for Pre-War Sports Cars.

Race winner Gareth Burnett in the 1931 Talbot 105 leads fourth place finisher Rüdiger Friedrichs (1933 Alvis Firefly 4.3) into Abbey corner.

SILVERSTONE CLASSIC 2017

July 28th. – July 30th.

A weekend of sunshine and showers did nothing to dampen the enthusiasm of the 100,000 spectators who packed the Northamptonshire circuit for the annual festival of 'Rocking and Racing' that is the Silverstone Classic.

With a packed programme of 22 races, featuring cars from over eight decades of motorsport; parade laps featuring McLarens, Jaguar XJ220s; high-speed demos by Williams F1 and World GP Bike Legends; together with incredible off-track entertainment, the weekend offered something for everyone.

Saturday's racing kicked off at 9:00am with Historic Formula Juniors (much to the surprise of the hare that, startled by the noise, suddenly emerged from the barrier at The Loop and looked for a minute as though it was going to join in!

Sam Wilson in a Lotus 20/22 out ran his competitors on a track still slippery from overnight rain to clinch the Formula Junior victory from Andrew Hibberd in second place. The 1-2 pairing of Wilson/Hibberd was repeated in the second Formula Junior race later on Saturday.

The following Historic Formula Ford race (in the 50th year of the series) was notable for the presence of ex-*Top Gear* and *Fifth Gear* presenter Tiff Needell in his 1971 Lotus 69F, a car in which he first raced in 1980 after winning it in a competition organised by Autosport magazine. No such luck in this race as he qualified 20th on the grid, with eventual winner Michael O'Brien taking the flag in his Merlyn MK20A, repeating the win in the second Formula Ford race on Sunday.

Pole-sitter Oliver Bryant's Lotus 15 was beaten off the line by Chris Ward (Lister Costin) in the Stirling Moss Trophy for Pre '61 Sports Cars. Ward then dominated the race, with Rob Barff (Lotus 15) taking second place after hard-charging Bryant retired.

Under 2-litre Touring Cars are always fun to watch, with wheel-lifting Minis and sideways Ford Lotus Cortinas (and the John Fitzpatrick Trophy race on Saturday didn't disappoint. Pole man Steve Soper (Ford Lotus Cortina) looked in line for the win until a late spin gifted the lead, and the race victory, to the similarly-mounted Mark Sumpter.

The Kidston Trophy race for pre-war sports cars saw a mighty tussle between Gareth Burnett in the 1931 Talbot 105 and the pole-sitting Wakeman/Blakeney-Edwards 1928 Frazer Nash, which ended in the Talbot's favour by just 0.162s.

Saturday's lunch-time diversions saw high-speed demonstrations by World GP Bike Riders including: Wayne Gardener, Freddie Spencer, Didier De Radigues, Niggi Schmassman, Freddie Sheene (son of Barry), Steve Parrish, Maria Costello and Remy Gardner. Plus demonstration laps by Nigel Mansell's 1992 Championship winning Williams FW14B, this being Williams' 40th year in Formula One and 25 years since Mansell's British GP win.

To celebrate the 25th anniversary of the Jaguar XJ220 over 40 examples took to the track for a parade lap, headed by the three cars that competed in the Le Mans 24 hour race in 1993.

The main event of the day, the FIA Masters Historic Formula One race, had newcomer Jonathan Kennard (who had never raced an F1 car before) on pole in the gold Warsteiner Arrows A3. Although he led from the start, Kennard eventually was passed by a charging Nick Padmore in the Williams FW07C and had to settle for second.

For a complete contrast qualifying for the Celebrity Challenge race in Austin A30/35s followed, after which we had to leave although racing continued into the (very wet) evening; but we returned on Sunday to another full programme, including the RAC Tourist Trophy.

Early leader James Cottingham in the DK Engineering E-Type was overhauled by Lucas Halusa in the Ferrari 250GT 'Breadvan', who then held a comfortable lead and, despite an unexplained loss of time late in the race, took the chequered flag ahead of the rapid Simon Hadfield who brought the Aston Martin DP212 up through the field from 17th to take second place from Patrick Blakeney-Edwards' Cobra in sight of the flag.

Halusa's victory was short-lived however as a 45 second penalty for exceeding the pitlane speed limit relegated the Ferrari to fifth and handed the win to Hadfield.

Blakeney-Edwards put in another stellar performance in the following race (the RAC Woodcote Trophy for pre '56 Sports Cars (with a win in the 1955 Cooper T38 shared with Fred Wakeman, taking the lead from the Pearson brothers D-type during the pit stops.

As John Pearson fell back in the closing stages of the race, second place was taken from him by Chris Ward in the JD Classics Cooper Jaguar T33.

The second Historic F1 race of the weekend saw Michael Lyons (1980 Williams FW07B) take the win from Nick Padmore (1981 Williams FW07C) and Jonathan Kennard (Arrows A3). Both races were therefore won by a Williams FW07 (the same car that gave Williams their first GP win here at Silverstone in 1979.

As on Saturday the following event was a complete contrast with the A30/35 owner/drivers taking their cars out for the second part of the Celebrity Challenge (the first part with actual celebrities having been run late on Saturday in very wet conditions with a probably predictable red flag result.

A three-way battle for the lead developed between James Colburn, Jonathan Lewis and Mike Jordan, with Jordan coming out on top at the end and the pursuing pair separated by just 0.002 seconds.

Both Celebrity Challenge races helped the event to raise a very significant amount of money for the Classic's official charity partner Prostate Cancer UK, and once the results were combined, it was the Bike Legends team that won.

For Jaguar enthusiasts the new Jaguar Classic Challenge was a must-watch with hordes of E-Types mixing it up with other Jaguar models from XK150s to Mk.1 and Mk.2 saloons.

The low-drag E-Type of Julian Thomas stole an early lead but a technical problem caused him to drop back down the field and eventually retire. Victory finally went to Gary Pearson from the fast-finishing James Dodd, both in E-Types.

The FIA Masters Historic Sports Cars race was a ding-dong (literally) battle which ended under the safety car with many damaged vehicles around the circuit.

Third man on the grid Martin O'Connell (Chevron B19) made a superb start to lead from pole sitter Paul Gibson (Lola T70), who battled with Nick Padmore for second until they touched, sending Padmore into the barriers.

Gibson and O'Connell then battled for the lead until a puncture ended Gibson's challenge. After the safety car was deployed nine minutes from the end O'Connell was assured of the win.

The last race before the rain came on Sunday was the Maserati Trophy for pre-1966 Grand Prix Cars. Motor Sport Magazine Driver of the Weekend Sam Wilson (three wins from four starts), and winner of Saturday's pre-'66 race, was on pole for this one in the Lotus 18 and straight into a thrilling race-long battle with Jon Fairley, resolved in Fairley's favour at the flag.

With the advent of heavy rain we decided it was time to head for home, so we missed the Group C race and the JET Super Touring Car Trophy, both of which by all accounts were exciting if somewhat damp.

Another fantastic weekend of classic racing, plus the opportunity to ogle the many interesting and unusual cars on the infield car club displays (according to the organisers around 10,000 of them!

Historic F1 cars in Parc Fermé

RAC TOURIST TROPHY

Martin and Lucas Halusa in the fabulous one-off Ferrari 250GT "Breadvan" took first place at the chequered flag in the Tourist Trophy race, only to be relegated to fifth after a 45 second penalty for exceeding the pit lane speed limit.

When Enzo Ferrari refused to sell Count Giovani Volpi a then-new Ferrari 250GTO for his Scuderia Serrenissima racing team Volpi commissioned engineer Giotto Bizzarrini to modify an ex-Ecurie Francorchamps 250GT. The revised bodywork of the modified car featured a sharply cut-off rear end that followed the theory of aerodynamicist Wunibald Kamm. The resulting Kamm-tail design quickly led to the car being dubbed the "Breadvan".

The car made its competition debut at the 1962 Le Mans 24 Hours driven by Carlo Abate and Colin Davis, where it was comfortably faster that the 250GTOs; but a broken driveshaft forced its retirement after four hours when in seventh position.

FIA MASTERS HISTORIC FORMULA ONE

John Surtees, the only man to win World Champion titles on both two and four wheels, founded the Surtees Racing Organisation to contest the newly formed CanAm Series becoming the Series' first champion that year driving a Lola T70.

After some success in Formula 5000 with their own-built car, the team entered Formula 1 in 1970 with Surtees as owner/driver.

After closing his eponymous racing team in 1970 Rob Walker brought his Brooke Bond Oxo sponsorship to Team Surtees and also managed Mike Hailwood, who drove this Surtees TS9 in 1971.

Swiss driver Philippe Scemama took the wheel at the 2017 Silverstone Classic.

FIA MASTERS HISTORIC FORMULA ONE

This unusual looking device is the Eifelland E21 campaigned by the Eifelland team in the 1972 F1 Season and driven by Rolf Stommelen.

Based on a March 721 with revised bodywork by the German industrial designer Luigi Colani featuring the air intake in front of the cockpit from which air is channelled around the cockpit to the engine, and with a single rear view mirror mounted centrally in front of the driver. Lack of downforce, overheating and reliability problems meant the car was not competitive, with two 10th place finishes being the car's best results in 1972.

Driven at Silverstone in 2017 by David Shaw to a class win in both FIA Masters Historic F1 races.

FIA MASTERS HISTORIC FORMULA ONE

Fittipaldi Automotive, formed by Wilson Fittipaldi and his younger brother Emerson in 1974, was the only F1 constructor to be based in Brazil; although the team later moved from São Paulo, Brazil to Reading in the UK.

Double World Champion Emerson made a surprise move for the 1978 season from McLaren to the Fittipaldi team, replacing his brother who took over team management, and scored the team's best result coming second in Brazil in the Fittipaldi F5A, while the team came seventh in the Constructor's Championship.

In 1980 future world champion Keke Rosberg scored a sensational podium finish in the Argentine GP in a later Fittipaldi F7.

Max Smith-Hilliard took the F5A to solid mid-field finishes in both FIA Masters Historic F1 races at the 2017 Classic.

FIA MASTERS HISTORIC FORMULA ONE

Jackie Stewart had won the 1969 World Championship with Ken Tyrrell's team driving a Ford Cosworth DFV-engined Matra MS80. After Matra's merger with Simca Tyrrell was asked to use Matra's own V12 engine; but Stewart judged it to be inferior to the DFV so Tyrrell purchased a March 701 chassis for the 1970 season.

Dissatisfied with the performance of the March chassis Tyrrell decided to build his own car designed in secret by Derek Gardner. The Tyrrell 001 made its F1 debut at the 1970 Canadian GP where Stewart took pole but retired with axle failure while in the lead. For the final two races of the 1970 season, USA and Mexico, Stewart led but retired in both races (in Watkins Glen an oil leak caused the engine to seize and in Mexico the suspension was damaged after running over a dog!

Thankfully no dogs escaped on to the track at Silverstone in 2017 where John Delane drove this Tyrrell 001.

FIA MASTERS HISTORIC FORMULA ONE

Joaquin Folch-Rusinol drove this Brabham BT49C to tenth in the first, and ninth in the second of the Historic F1 races over the weekend.

The Gordon Murray designed BT49C used hydropneumatic suspension to overcome the minimum ride height requirement by automatically lowering the car at speed. The system was later abandoned after it repeatedly jammed and was replaced with a more conventional set up.

The BT49C was introduced at the US GP West in Long Beach on March 15 1981 driven by Nelson Piquet and Hector Rebaque. Piquet finished third at that race and with consistently high finishes, including two more wins at the San Marino and German GPs, he took the first of his three World Champion titles by one point from Carlos Reutemann in the Williams FW07C.

FIA MASTERS HISTORIC FORMULA ONE

Jason Wright at the wheel of the Shadow DN8. The Shadow DN8 made its race debut at the 1976 Dutch GP where Tom Pryce qualified the car third on the grid and finished the race in fourth behind Hunt, Regazzoni and Andretti. Mid-field finishes followed in Italy and Canada with retirements in USA and Japan.

For the 1977 season the team fielded two DN8s for Pryce and Renzo Zorzi until Pryce was tragically killed at the South African GP. His replacement Alan Jones finished in the points at the Monaco and Belgian GPs and won in Austria (Shadow's one and only F1 victory).

The slow Zorzi was replaced by Ricard Patrese after five races; but with Patrese's best finish being ninth at Monaco he finished the season with just one championship point.

FIA MASTERS HISTORIC SPORTS CARS .

1963 Cooper Monaco King Cobra driven by Keith Ahlers and James Behlinger.

In the early 1960s Carroll Shelby had racing successes with his Shelby Cobras, based on an AC Ace chassis with a Ford V8 engine; but realised they would not be competitive in the new SCCA Can-Am series.

Realising the potential of the Cooper T61 Monaco, Shelby approached John Cooper who agreed to supply four modified T61 chassis to which Shelby fitted the Ford 289 4.7 litre V8. Weighing a mere 1300lb (590kg) and developing 270bhp the King Cobra was immediately competitive and won the 1964 Riverside Times Grand Prix in the hands of Parnelli Jones.

Pressure from Ford to develop the GT40 programme led Shelby to cease the King Cobra project after 1964 and the cars were sold to private buyers.

2017

FIA MASTERS HISTORIC SPORTS CARS.

After being pushed out of the gravel trap at Farm (inset), the 1971 Chevron B16 of Ross Hyett scatters gravel (off the racing line) up to The Loop while the 1970 Cooper Monaco T61M driven by Chris Jolly and Steve Farthing exits Aintree corner in the background.

FIA MASTERS HISTORIC SPORTS CARS.

From third on the grid Martin O'Connell in the Chevron B19 (#4) took the lead at the end of the first lap from Dan Gibson in the Lola T70 (#48). The pair stayed like that for the first ten laps until their pit stops, after which they resumed their battle at the front until Gibson fell away leaving O'Connell to take the win.

FIA MASTERS HISTORIC SPORTS CARS.

The Chevron B8 of Alec Hammond and Brian Johnson suffers major bodywork damage prior to its retirement on lap four.

Having built and raced his own Clubmans Formula cars Derek Bennett founded Derek Bennett Engineering Ltd in 1966 to build Chevron cars initially for GT racing and later for Formula 3 and 2. Bennett was killed in a hang-gliding accident in 1978, after which the company went into decline and folded in 1980.

The B8 was probably Chevron's most popular GT car with 44 examples built between 1968 and 1970, winning many racers in the hands of numerous drivers, including Stirling Moss. Moss owned and raced a B8, in which he famously beat Richard Attwood driving a Porsche 917 at Phoenix Park, Dublin in 1982.

FIA MASTERS HISTORIC SPORTS CARS

Trevor Fiorre designed this pretty little Elva GT160 with a 2 litre dry-sump BMW engine. Intended to go into production but only three prototypes were built, one of which was purchased by Richard Wrottesley who entered it for the 1965 Le Mans with Tony Lanfranchi as his co-driver. The car lasted for four hours before retiring with clutch problems.

Michael Birch drove the car at the 2017 Silverstone Classic.

FIA MASTERS HISTORIC SPORTS CARS

Charlie Birkett and James Littejohn drove this 1966 Ford GT40 to a solid mid-field finish in the Historic Sports Car race.

Ford's GT40 programme began after Henry Ford was rebuffed by Enzo Ferrari in 1963 negotiations for Ford to buy Ferrari. The GT40 developed from the Lola Mk 6, and went on to beat Ferrari at Le Mans in 1966 in a 1-2-3 finish for Ford, with Bruce McLaren and Chris Amon driving the winning car.

Further wins at Le Mans followed in 1967 (Dan Gurney/AJ Foyt) in the later Mk. IV version, 1968 (Pedro Rodriguez/Lucien Bianchi), and 1969 (Jacky Ickx/Jackie Oliver).

COMMANDER YORKE TROPHY

Sam Wilson (53) and Andrew Hibberd (79) finished first and second in both Commander Yorke Trophy races for Historic Formula Junior. Wilson's 1961 Lotus 20/22 is one year older than the Lotus 22 driven by Hibberd.

The Lotus 20 was announced at the 1961 Racing Car Show and works drivers Trevor Taylor and Peter Arundell took fifteen wins between them in that season. Jo Bonnier also won seven times driving a Lotus 20 for Ecurie Romande the same year.

COMMANDER YORKE TROPHY

The Gemini Mk2 Formula Junior cars were constructed by Chequered Flag Engineering, a new company formed by Graham Warner of famous sports car sales company *The Chequered Flag* based in Chiswick High Road, London. The Gemini evolved from the Morland Mk2, a Formula Junior car designed by Len Terry and constructed by Leslie Redmond in 1959, which Warner had purchased.

The Gemini Mk 2 made its competition debut at Brands Hatch in October 1959 and around 30 were produced in total, four with Ford Cosworth engines and the rest with BMC A Series power.

James Owen drove the car at Silverstone in 2017 to mid-field finishes in both Historic Formula junior races.

STIRLING MOSS TROPHY

This weird looking machine is *Old Yeller 2,* a Buick-engined special built in 1959 by Max and Ina Balchowsky at their famous Hollywood Motors Shop in Los Angeles, and driven in the early 1960s by Max, as well as drivers to become famous later such as Dan Gurney, Carroll Shelby and Bob Bondurant.

Old Yeller 2 is now owned, and was driven in the Stirling Moss Trophy for pre-1961 Sports Cars, by Ernie Nagamatsu who has driven the car at Historic racing events in the USA, England, Australia and New Zealand.

STIRLING MOSS TROPHY

In 1964, inspired by the Ferrari 250GT "Breadvan", Lotus XI owner Graham Capel had the bodywork of his car altered to follow the same aerodynamic principles.

The resulting Lotus XI GT, was raced at Silverstone this year by Brian Palmer, who seems to have been involved in an argument with another car judging by the amount of 'racer tape' holding the door on.

JOHN FITZPATRICK TROPHY

From the days when BMW made good-looking, well proportioned cars this smart 1965 1800 Ti driven by Stuart Patterson and Warren Dunbar made a welcome change to the hordes of Lotus Cortinas in the John Fitzpatrick Trophy race for under 2 litre Touring Cars.

Credited with putting BMW on the path to success the 4-door BMW saloons first appeared at the 1961 Frankfurt Motor show in 1500 guise, to be followed two years later by the 1800 and the twin carburettor 1800 Ti.

Early competition success for the works 1800 Ti included a seventh place overall and class win at the 1964 Nürburgring 6 Hour race in the hands of Hubert Hahne and Anton Fischhaber. Hahne and Heinz Eppelein followed that a month later with an overall win in the 12 hour event at the same circuit. Hahne also won the German national championship that year.

JOHN FITZPATRICK TROPHY

Augusto and Ambrogio Perfetti brought their Lotus Cortina home in second place behind the winning Lotus Cortina driven by Mark Sumpter.

MASERATI TROPHY FOR HGPCA PRE-1966 GRAND PRIX CARS

Marc Valvekens' Aston Martin DBR4/4 (#16) leads the Scirocco F1 63 driven by Paul Woolley (#129).

ASTON MARTIN DBR4/4

Following their successes in sports car racing Aston Martin wanted to repeat that in Formula One with the DBR4/4 designed in 1957 by Aston's chief race car designer Ted Cutting. Unfortunately the demands of Aston's sports car programme led to a protracted development period and the car did not appear on track until 1959, by which time much of its technology was outdated.

Although the car's debut at the non-championship BRDC International Trophy race in May 1959 showed promise with works drivers Roy Salvadori and Carroll Shelby finishing second and sixth respectively, their championship appearances were less successful. Both cars retired in the Dutch GP when their engine blew and the best results were sixth place for Salvadori in both the British and Portuguese Grands Prix.

SCIROCCO F1

In 1962 Americans Tony Settember and Hugh Powell ran the revamped Emeryson F1 team under the name of Scirocco-Powell Racing. For the 1963 season an entirely new car, the Scirocco F1, was designed using the BRM V8 engine and finished in the USA racing colours of white and blue.

One car was ready for its F1 debut at the notoriously rain-affected 1963 Belgian GP driven by Settember; but failed to finish when it crashed out during an horrendous rain storm. By the British GP a second car had been completed which was driven by Ian Burgess but both cars retired with engine trouble. The best result for Scirocco was Settember's second place at the non-championship Austrian GP and the team folded at the end of the 1963 season.

2017

MASERATI TROPHY FOR HGPCA PRE-1966 GRAND PRIX CARS

First and fourth place finishers, Sam Wilson in the Lotus 18 (#118) and Jon Fairley's Brabham BT11/19 (#11) line up to pass the Lotus 18/21 of Erik Staes.

The Brabham BT11 was campaigned by the Brabham Racing Organisation in 1964 and 1965, with their best results being two consecutive second places in the 1965 USA and Mexican GPs for Dan Gurney.

Gurney was probably the tallest person to drive in Formula One at 6'4" (193cm) and the Ford Mk. IV that he drove to victory with AJ Foyt at Le Mans in 1967 had to be modified with the famous 'Gurney Bubble' to accommodate his helmet. It was at that race that Gurney spontaneously sprayed Champagne around on the podium, starting a motorsport tradition that continues to this day.

CELEBRITY CHALLENGE TROPHY

Teams of Olympic Gold Medalists, TV & Radio stars, motorbike legends, big names on the music scene and a dedicated Sky Sports team battled it out in Austin A30s and A35s to raise money for Prostate Cancer UK, the 2017 Classic's official chosen charity.

Battling for second and third place honours in the second race are James Colburn (#121) and Jonathan Lewis, with Colburn finishing ahead of Lewis by 0.891 seconds.

Introduced in 1951, the Austin A30 and later A35, soon attracted the attention of tuning companies, with such later luminaries as Graham Hill cutting their motor racing teeth behind the wheel of the diminutive Austin.

CELEBRITY CHALLENGE TROPHY

Mike Jordan took the win in the second race for the Rocking & Racing team in this Austin A30 which was driven in the first race by Howard Donald from *Take That*.

RAC TOURIST TROPHY

Wolfgang Friedrichs and Simon Hadfield took this Aston Martin DP212 to a fine win from pole position.

The DP212 was a one-off project built to return Aston Martin to Le Mans in 1962, driven by Graham Hill and Richie Ginther. Hill was first away at the traditional Le Mans start and led at the end of the first lap. A piston failure forced its retirement from ninth place after six hours.

Although fast the DP212 suffered from high speed stability problems, which led to a later redesign featuring a more aerodynamic 'Kamm' tail. Mike Salmon successfully campaigned the car in the 1970s, winning the HSCC Classic Sports Car Championship in 1974.

2017

RAC TOURIST TROPHY

The Lotus Elites of Michael Gans (#28) and John Davison (#36) enjoyed a virtually race-long duel to finish in 11th and 13th respectively, even though Gans collected a 45 second penalty for speeding in the pit lane.

Conforming to Colin Chapman's philosophy of "adding lightness", the Elite featured an innovative glass-reinforced plastic monocoque into which a steel subframe was bonded to carry the 1.2 litre Coventry Climax FWE engine. The combination of lightweight with good aerodynamics gave the Elite outstanding performance; but the novel body construction and some highly stressed components led to reliability issues (maybe the source of the old adage that LOTUS stood for 'Lots Of Trouble, Usually Serious'?). Over 1000 Elites were sold during the production run from 1958-1963, but it was rumoured that Lotus lost £100 on every one.

The car's competition record is outstanding however. Jim Clark's long association with Lotus began when he raced an Elite at the Brands Hatch Boxing Day meeting in 1958 finishing second to another Elite driven by Lotus boss Colin Chapman. Clark also drove an Elite at Le Mans in 1959, finishing tenth overall and fifth in the Index of Thermal Efficiency, a category in which Elites were very successful over the following years.

Race 1: Commander Yorke Trophy for Historic Formula Junior
First: Sam Wilson (Lotus20/22))
Second: Andrew Hibberd (Lotus 22)
Third: Westie Mitchell (De Tomaso 63)

Race 2: Formula Ford 50 presented by Historic Motorsport International
First: Michael O'Brien (Merlyn Mk20A)
Second: Ed Thurston (Elden Mk8)
Third: Max Bartell (Merlyn Mk20A)

Race 3: Stirling Moss Trophy for Pre '61 Sports Cars
First: Chris Ward (Lister Costin)
Second: Rob Barff (Lotus 15)
Third: Richard Kent (Lister Costin Jaguar)

Race 4: John Fitzpatrick Trophy for Under 2 Litre Touring Cars
First: Mark Sumpter (Ford Lotus Cortina)
Second: Ambrogio Perfetti/Augusto Perfetti (Ford Lotus Cortina)
Third: Karl Jones/Chris Ward (Ford Lotus Cortina)

Race 5: Kidston Trophy for Pre-War Sports Cars
First: Gareth Burnett (Talbot 105)
Second: Frederic Wakeman/Patrick Blakeney-Edwards (Frazer Nash Super Sports)
Third: Charles Gillett/Eddie Williams (Frazer Nash TT Rep)

Race 6: Commander Yorke Trophy for Historic Formula Junior
First: Sam Wilson (Lotus20/22) 9 laps
Second: Andrew Hibberd (Lotus 22)
Third: Tim De Silva (Brabham BT2)

Race 7: FIA Masters Historic Formula One
First: Nick Padmore (Williams FW07C)
Second: Jonathan Kennard (Arrows A3)
Third: Michael Lyons (Williams FW07B)

Race 8: Maserati Trophy for Pre 1966 Grand Prix Cars
First: Sam Wilson (Lotus 18 372)
Second: Jon Fairley (Brabham BT11/19)
Third: William Nuthall (Cooper T53)

Race 9: JET Super Touring Car Trophy
First: Jason Minshaw (Volvo S40)
Second: Jon Minshaw (Audi A4)
Third: Dave Jarman (Nissan Primera)

Race 10: Silverstone Classic Celebrity Challenge Trophy (Pro Class)
First: Steve Soper (Austin A35)
Second: Martin Donnelly (Austin A35)
Third: Mark Blundell (Austin A35)
(Amateur Class)
First: Neil Primrose (Austin A35)
Second: Tony Jardine (Austin A30)
Third: Jason Kenny (Austin A35)

Race 11: Gallet International Trophy for Classic GT Cars (Pre 1966)
First: Oliver Bryant (AC Cobra)
Second: Roger Wills (Bizzarrini 5300 GT)
Third: Andrew Haddon (AC Cobra)

Race 12: Group C
First: Steve Tandy (Spice SE90 GTP)
Second: Mike Wrigley (Spice SE89C)
Third: Tony Sinclair (Spice SE90C)

Race 13: Formula Ford 50 presented by Historic Motorsport International
First: Michael O'Brien (Merlyn Mk20A)
Second: Callum Grant (Merlyn Mk20A)
Third: Benn Tilley (Merlyn Mk20A)

Race 14: Royal Automobile Club Tourist Trophy for Historic Cars (Pre 1963 GT)
First: Wolfgang Friedrichs/Simon Hadfield (Aston Martin DP212)
Second: Martin Hunt/Pat Blakeney-Edwards (AC Cobra)
Third: James Cottingham/Harvey Stanley (Jaguar E-type)

Race 15: Royal Automobile Club Woodcote Trophy for Pre 1956 Sports Cars
First: Fred Wakeman/Pat Blakeney-Edwards (Cooper T38)
Second: Andrew Smith/Chris Ward (Cooper Jaguar T33)
Third: Gary Pearson/John Pearson (Jaguar D-Type)

Race 16: FIA Masters Historic Formula One
First: Michael Lyons (Williams FW07B)
Second: Nick Padmore (Williams FW07C)
Third: Jonathan Kennard (Arrows A3)

Race 17: Silverstone Classic Celebrity Challenge Trophy (Owners)
First: Mike Jordan (Austin A30)
Second: James Colburn (Austin A30)
Third: Jonathan Lewis (Austin A35)

Race 18: Jaguar Classic Challenge
First: Gary Pearson (Jaguar E-Type)
Second: Graeme Dodd/James Dodd (Jaguar E-Type)
Third: Ben Short (Jaguar E-Type)

Race 19: FIA Masters Historic Sports Cars
First: Martin O'Connell (Chevron B19)
Second: Rob Garofall/Philip Hall (Lola T212)
Third: Andrew Banks/Max Banks (McLaren M6B)

Race 20: Maserati Trophy for Pre 1966 Grand Prix Cars
First: Jon Fairley (Brabham BT11/19)
Second: Sam Wilson (Lotus 18 372)
Third: Barry Cannell (Brabham BT11A)

Race 21: Group C
First: Kriton Lendoudis (Mercedes C11)
Second: Steve Tandy (Spice SE90 GTP)
Third: Philippe Scemama (Spice SE89C) + 48.353S

Race 22: JET Super Touring Car Trophy
First: James Dodd (Honda Accord)
Second: Jason Minshaw (Volvo S40)
Third: Darren Fielding (Ford Mondeo)

**RACE 7: START OF THE 2017 FIA MASTERS
HISTORIC FORMULA ONE RACE.**

Pole sitter Jonathan Kennard (#84 - Arrows A3) leads Michael Lyons
(#50 - WilliamsFW07B), eventually race winner Nick Padmore (#1 -
Williams FW07C), and Andy Wolfe (#13- Tyrrell)

RAC Tourist Trophy race for Historic Pre-1963 GT Cars. Muscular Austin Healey 3000 of Alex Bell ahead of dainty Lotus Elites of John Davison (#177) and Michael Gans (#28) emerge through the exhaust heat haze into Copse corner.

SILVERSTONE CLASSIC 2018

July 20th. – July 22nd.

Another 100,000+ crowd sizzled under exceedingly un-British hot sunshine (apart from Friday evening) at the 2018 Silverstone Classic weekend and enjoyed a packed programme of historic racing from Formula Junior to Formula 1.

Since the Silverstone Classic first started back in 1990 it has gone from strength to strength with Tiff Needell even describing it recently as "The Glastonbury of Motorsport". With a whole range of activities and attractions on offer, including displays by over 100 car clubs across the infield area, plus live music on the Friday and Saturday nights (Soul II Soul, and UB40 headlining this year) you can see what he means. For us however the main attraction is the cars and the racing, so we'll concentrate on that for this report.

Due to other commitments we couldn't make the Friday qualifying day this year, so we rocked up bright and early on Saturday in our recently acquired MG TF under slightly overcast skies, although that soon changed!

The first thing to strike us was that the VIP/Media shuttle service this year was courtesy of Tesla Model S and Model X cars owned by members of the Tesla Owners Club. We took advantage of this to get a lift in a Model S to The Wing and had an interesting conversation with the owner who was full of praise for the car, even though in 36 months of Tesla ownership various problems meant he'd only had the actual car he bought for 12 of those months.

After telling us how cheap it was to run (a round trip to Scotland had cost less than £10 in charging top-ups. "That would have been at least £100 in petrol", he said (he gave us a quick demonstration of the phenomenal acceleration from rest that electric motors delivering 100% torque from the word go can provide. "It'll do that all the way to 100mph!" was his parting remark. Looks like the all-electric future is going to be fun after all.

Saturdays on-track action began with the Jim Clark Trophy race for 1958-1960 Formula Junior cars, won by Will Mitcham in a 1960 U2 Mk.2 from Chris Drake's Terrier Mk. 4.

The second race of the day was more our style featuring pre-1963 GT cars in the RAC Tourist Trophy, where the bare metal, unpainted and raucous sounding AC Cobra of Martin Hunt and Patrick Blakeney-Edwards took a well-deserved win from the two E-Types of James Cottingham/Harvey Stanley, and Sam Hancock/Gregor Fisken.

More thundering action followed with the Stirling Moss Trophy for pre-1961 Sportscars which brought out a field of D-Types, Lister Knobblies, Cooper Monacos, Lotus Elevens and Fifteens, and various Lolas.

The Lister Knobblies of Chris Ward and Tony Wood/Will Nuthall took the first two spots after 20 laps from third placed man Roger Wills in a Lotus 15.

The second of the day's Formula Junior races, the Denny Hulme Trophy for 1961-1963 cars, resulted in victory for Sam Wilson in a 1961 Lotus 20/22 from Timothy De Silva (1962 Brabham BT2), with Jonathan Milicevic (Merlyn Mk5/7) taking the third place spot.

During the racing lunch break the crowds were entertained by high speed demo laps from World GP Bike Legends and Legends of Modern Formula One, followed by a parade of retro motorcycles celebrating the 80th anniversary of the Ace Café and a number of car parades celebrating anniversaries including 50 years of the Morgan Plus 8 while the Aston Martin Owners' Club marked the 70th and 60th anniversaries of the DB1 and DB4 respectively.

Opening the afternoon racing was the highlight of the day, the FIA Masters Historic Formula One race, which saw pole man Nick Padmore in his ex-Carlos Reutemann 1981 Williams FW07C score an emphatic win over second place on the grid MIchael Lyons in the Penthouse branded Hesketh 308E, with Belgian driver Christophe D'Ansembourg securing third place in another Williams FW07C.

In the following race for HSCC Road Sports (1947-1979) John Davison took the chequered flag in his nimble Lotus Elan S, ahead of a pair of Morgan Plus 8s driven by Richard Plant and Jonathan Edwards.

A red flag in the Adrian Flux Trophy race for pre 1966 GP cars brought a premature end to an exciting four-way battle, with the win taken by Will Nuthall (1960 Cooper T53) ahead of the 1961 Lotus18/21 of Peter Horsman and Tim de Silva's 1962 Lotus 24.

Tin-top fans had something to shout about in the JET Super Touring Car Trophy when 1989 British Touring Car Champion Rickard Rydell looked to be on target for a win from pole position in the Volvo S40 in which he became Champion, only to be beaten to the line by James Dodd in a Honda Accord from the same year.

The last three races of the day were entitled *Daytona at Dusk* and began at 6:00pm with the International Trophy for Classic (pre-1966) GT cars. BTCC racer Jake Hill put in an outstanding performance to bring Richard Wheeler's Lotus Elan home first, using every bit of the Elan's agility to hold of the hard-charging Gans/Wolfe AC Cobra, with John Spiers' 1965 TVR Griffith in third at the flag.

We had to leave after so missed the last two races but can report that the Yokohama Trophy for FIA Masters Historic Sports Cars was won by Oliver Bryant (Lola T70 Mk38), and Steve Tandy brought the Lola B12/60 home first in the Masters Endurance Legends race to end the day's track action.

Tin-Top Sunday saw touring cars dominant with four of the ten races devoted to the hot saloons. The first race however saw Sam Wilson lift the Jochen Rindt Trophy for Formula Junior (1961-1963) cars with his second win of the weekend, ahead of a storming performance by Cameron Jackson who brought the 1962 Brabham BT2 home in second after starting 50th on the grid.

Second race of the day, the RAC Woodcote Trophy for pre-1956 Sportscars saw Garry Pearson sweep to victory in the 1955 Jaguar D-Type ahead of the Wakeman/Blakeney-Edwards Cooper T38, with the Wilson/Stretton Maserati 250S taking third spot.

The smaller tin-tops were out next in the Gallet Trophy for under 2-litre Touring Cars in which Rob Huff (2012 WTC Champion) shared Andy Wolfe's 1965 Lotus Cortina to take the chequered flag just 16 seconds ahead of the Alfaholics-entered Alfa Romeo Giulia Sprint GTA of Andy and Maxim Banks, with the Brown/Dutton Lotus Cortina taking third.

In the Historic Touring Car Challenge, father and son Nick and Harry Whale dominated the field in one of the iconic BMW M3 E30s, with another of these successful saloon cars, that of Mark Smith and Arran Moulton-Smith, taking second ahead of the 3-litre Ford Capri of Ric Wood.

Nick Padmore, despite starting from a reversed eighth on the grid, in Sunday's FIA Masters Historic F1 race, charged to the front of the field to secure his second win of the weekend.

Michael Lyons was again second spot on the podium, while his audacious pass on Martin Stretton's Tyrrell around the outside at Stowe on Saturday made him the first recipient of the Henry Hope-Frost #FEVER Award. Created in honour of the broadcaster and journalist, who died in a road accident earlier this year, the #FEVER Award recognises the driver who produced the most memorable high-octane moment from the weekend.

Sunday's JET Super Touring Car Trophy race was pretty much a repeat of Saturday's with the battle for the lead between Rickard Rydell and James Dodd again resolved in Dodd's favour at the flag, with 1989 and 1995 champion John Cleland in the Vauxhall Vectra taking the last step on the podium.

Endurance racers took to the track again on Sunday with Steve Tandy repeating his win from the previous evening in the ex-Dyson Racing Lola B12/60 after a race-long tussle with Herve Regout driving the Lola Aston Martin DBR1-2. Third place, and the Scarf & Googles Award for the most admired competition car at the Classic, went to the Peugeot 908 driven by David Porter.

With the sun beating down I made a strategic retreat from a hot track-side to the cooler shade of the grandstand at Luffield for the Adrian Flux Trophy second race in which Saturday's second place finisher Peter Horsman drove his Lotus 18/21 to victory, followed by Mark Daniel (Cooper T45) with Tony Wood's front-engined Maserati Tec Mec clinching the third place.

American muscle cars took to the track in the last race of the weekend, the Transatlantic Trophy for pre-1966 Touring Cars in which Andy Wolfe scored his second victory of the day sharing a 1964 Ford Falcon Sprint with Mike Gardiner. The Ford Mustangs of Craig Davies and James Thorpe/Sean McInerney completed the podium line-up.

PJO

2018

Hectic first lap of the last race of the 2017 Classic weekend, the Transatlantic Trophy for pre-1966 Touring Cars.

The front runners have escaped our lens, but this mid-field bunch is led by American muscle in the form of the Ford Falcon Sprint (#88) driven by Jason Minshaw and Martin Melling, ahead of the Ford Galaxie (#263) of Bill Shepherd, with a closely bunched field behind.

Andrea Stortoni's Lotus Cortina kicks up the dust on the way to a first lap retirement.

FIA MASTERS HISTORIC FORMULA ONE

In searing heat Nick Padmore drove the 1981 Williams FW07C to victory in both Historic F1 races at the 2018 Silverstone Classic.

Williams won the 1981 F1 Constructors Championship with Alan Jones and Carlos Reutemann driving, however Reutemann lost the driver's championship by one point to Nelson Piquet (Brabham BT49C).

FIA MASTERS HISTORIC FORMULA ONE

The Shadow DN5 which Jean-Pierre Jarier drove in 1975 had Gregor Fisken behind the wheel at the 2018 Silverstone Classic.

At the 1975 F1 opening round in Argentina Jarier took pole with a spectacular qualifying drive, but he did not start the race as the car came to a halt just metres from the pits on his warm up lap with a stripped crown wheel and pinion – newly fitted by the team after qualifying as a precaution!

At the following race in Brazil Jarier again put the DN5 on pole, and also recorded fastest lap in the race, but retired after 32 laps when the fuel metering unit seized.

FIA MASTERS HISTORIC FORMULA ONE

Michael Lyons drove this Hesketh 308E to second place after Nick Padmore in Saturday's Historic F1 race, and repeated the performance in Sunday's race.

When at the end of 1975 Lord Hesketh could no longer financially support the un-sponsored Hesketh Team, Anthony 'Bubbles' Horsley kept the name alive in F1 with, at the time controversial, sponsorship in 1977 from Penthouse and Rizla, and Olympus Cameras in 1978.

The team's best result in those two years was a seventh place at the 1977 Austrian GP by Rupert Keegan. Other drivers included Harald Ertl, Davina Galica and Eddie Cheever but the team scored no points in 1978, their last year.

FIA MASTERS HISTORIC FORMULA ONE

Paul Tattersal did not finish in Saturday's Historic F1 race but brought this Ensign N179 home on Sunday.

For the 1979 season Ensign was funded by Hong Kong millionaire Theodore 'Teddy' Yip and the N179, designed by Dave Baldwin, initially appeared with probably the ugliest nose of any F1 car which had three radiators stacked vertically in front of the driver.

Drivers through 1979 were Derek Daly, Patrick Gaillard and Marc Surer, but Gaillard was the only one to finish a race with a 13th place in the British GP at Silverstone.

HISTORIC TOURING CAR CHALLENGE

Race-winning 1989 BMW M3 E30 driven by Nick and Harry Whale, passes the 1980 Rover SD1 of Martin Overington and Guy Stevens into Village corner.

The controversial World Touring Car Championship of 1987 was won by Roberto Ravaglia driving a Schnitzer Motorsport BMW M3; but only after protests against the Eggenberger Ford RS500s in the Bathurst 1000 race were upheld and the cars subsequently disqualified. In that year's European Touring Car Championship Winfried Vogt took the title driving a Linder Rennsport BMW M3. In 1988 Frank Sytner won the British Touring Car Championship driving a Prodrive-prepared BMW M3.

David Price Racing built the Group 2 Unipart sponsored Rover SD1 that appeared at the 1980 Tourist Trophy race at Silverstone (Round 8 of that year's European Touring Car Championship) driven by Jeff Allam and Tiff Needell. Although setting fast times in practice and making seventh on the grid, an engine problem sidelined the car after 62 laps of the 500km race.

HISTORIC TOURING CAR CHALLENGE

First lap action. The Jaguar XJ12 C Broadspeed (#144) driven by Paul Pochciol and James Hanson takes the lead from third on the grid, followed by the pole sitting, and eventual winning, BMW of Nick and Harry Whale (#66) and the Ford Sierra Cosworth of Julian Thomas and Callum Lockie (#101) which did not finish.

The BMW of Tom Houlbrook and the Rover SD1 of Ken Clarke/Matt Jackson get sideways in the background.

ADRIAN FLUX TROPHY

In this race for pre-1966 Grand Prix Cars, Peter Horsman took this 1961 Lotus 18/21 to second place in the race on Saturday and a win in Sunday's race.

The Lotus 18/21 was a re-bodied version of the slab-sided Lotus 18 produced for sale to privateers (the Lotus works team used the updated Lotus 21).

This particular car is powered by the 2.5 litre Coventry Climax engine which was fitted to cars shipped down under to compete in the Tasman Series.

2018

ADRIAN FLUX TROPHY

A trio of Coopers from different eras. Leading is the front-engined 1952 Cooper Bristol Mk 1 driven by Barry Wood, followed by the mid-engined 1957 Cooper T43 with John Busey at the wheel. At the rear is another 1952 Cooper Bristol driven by Niamh Wood.

2018

Olympic cycling champion Chris Hoy at the wheel of the 2007 Courage LC75 that was also driven by Mike Furness.

French racing driver Yves Courage began his long association with the Le Mans 24 Hours in 1981 when he and Jean-Phillipe Grand drove a Lola T298, with the pairing finishing in 18th place. The following year he founded Courage Compétition, constructing his own cars to contest Le Mans and other endurance races, with the first car being the C01 powered by a Ford Cosworth DFL. This was entered for the 1982 Le Mans driven by Courage/Grand who were joined by Michel Dubois; but the transmission failed after 78 laps.

Courage Compétition's best results at Le Mans were a third in 1987, where Courage shared the driving of a C20/Porsche with Pierrie-Henri Raphanel and Hervé Regout, and 1995 when Bob Wollek, Eric Hélary and Mario Andretti brought a C34/Porsche home in second place. Courage also sold chassis to other teams, notably Pescarolo whose Judd-powered C60 chassis cars came second and fifth at Le Mans in 2006.

The LC75 introduced in 2007 to contest the LMP2 class is powered by the 2-litre turbocharged AER P07 engine and made its debut at that year's Monza 100 kms, where it finished 27th and 4th in class in the hands of Alain Filhol, Bruce Jouanny and Jacques Nicolet.

Noël del Bello Racing entered LC75 (#24) for the 2007 Le Mans driven by the international trio of Vitaly Petrov (Russia), Romain Ianetta (France) and Liz Halliday (USA). The car lasted 198 laps before a gearshift problem forced the car's retirement.

142

MASTERS ENDURANCE LEGENDS

Steve Tandy was first to the chequered flag in both the Saturday and Sunday Masters Endurance Legends races in this Lola B12/60. Originally campaigned by Dyson Racing in the 2013 American Le Mans series, and powered by a turbocharged 2.0 litre Mazda engine.

In Europe Rebellion Racing used the Lola B12/60 but with a naturally aspirated Toyota V8. These were the only two customers for the B12/60 before Lola ceased trading in 2012.

Race **Jim Clark Trophy for Historic Formula Junior (1958-1960)**
First: Will Mitcham (U2 Mk2)
Second: Christopher Drake (Terrier Mk 4 Series 1)
Third: Marcus Griffiths (Lotus 18

Race 2: **Royal Automobile Club Tourist Trophy for Historic Cars (Pre 1963 GT)**
First: Martin Hunt/Patrick Blakeney-Edwards (AC Cobra)
Second: James Cottingham/Harvey Stanley (Jaguar E-Type)
Third: Gregor Fisken/Sam Hancock (Jaguar E-Type)

Race 3: **Stirling Moss Trophy for Pre 1961 Sports Cars**
First: Chris Ward (Lister Knobbly)
Second: Tony Wood/Will Nuthall (Lister Knobbly)
Third: Roger Wills (Lotus 15)

Race 4: **Denny Hulme Trophy for Historic Formula Junior (1961-1963)**
First: Sam Wilson (Lotus 20/22)
Second: Timothy De Silva (Brabham BT2)
Third: Jonathan Milicevic (Merlyn Mk5/7)

Race 5: **FIA Masters Historic Formula One**
First: Nick Padmore (Williams FW07C)
Second: Michael Lyons (Hesketh 308E)
Third: Christophe D'Ansembourg (Williams FW07C)

Race 6: **HSCC Road Sports (1947-1979)**
First: John Davison (Lotus Elan S1)
Second: Richard Plant (Morgan Plus 8)
Third: Jonathan Edwards (Morgan Plus 8)

Race : **Adrian Flux Trophy for Pre 1966 Grand Prix Cars**
First: William Nuthall (Cooper T53)
Second: Peter Horsman (Lotus 18/21)
Third: Timothy de Silva (Lotus 24)

Race 8: **JET Super Touring Car Trophy**
First: James Dodd (Honda Accord)
Second: Rickard Rydell (Volvo S40)
Third: Jason Hughes (Vauxhall Vectra)

Race 9: **Daytona at Dusk, International Trophy for Classic GT Cars (Pre 1966)**
First: Jake Hill (Lotus Elan)
Second: Michael Gans/Andy Wolfe (AC Cobra)
Third: John Spiers (TVR Griffith)

Race 10: **Daytona at Dusk, Yokohama Trophy for FIA Masters Historic Sports Cars**
First: Oliver Bryant (Lola T70 Mk38)
Second: Michael Gans (Lola T290)
Third: Diogo Ferro/Martin Stretton (Lola T292)

Race 11: **Daytona at Dusk, Masters Endurance Legends**
First: Steve Tandy (Lola B12/60)
Second: Christophe D'Ansembourg (Lola Aston DBR1-2)
Third: Martin Short (Dallara SP1)

HISTORIC TOURING CAR CHALLENGE WITH TONY DRON TROPHY

Mark Burnett's Mini 1275GT lifts a rear wheel around The Loop.

Race 12: **Jochen Rindt Trophy for Historic Formula Junior (1961-1963)**

First: Sam Wilson (Lotus 20/22)
Second: Cameron Jackson(Brabham BT2)
Third: Peter Morton (Lightning Envoyette)

Race 13: **RAC Woodcote Trophy for pre 1956 Sportscars**

First: Gary Pearson (Jaguar D-Type)
Second: Frederic Wakeman/Patrick Blakeney-Edwards (Cooper T38)
Third: Richard Wilson/Martin Stretton (Maserati 250S)

Race14: **Gallett Trophy for Under 2-litre Touring Cars**

First: Andy Wolfe/Robb Huff (Ford Lotus Cortina)
Second: Andrew & Maxim Banks (Alfa Romeo Giulia Sprint GTA)
Third: Richard Dutton/Neil Brown (Ford Lotus Cortina)

Race 15: **John Surtees Trophy for Historic Formula Junior (1958-1960**

First: Andrew Hibberd (Lola Mk.2)
Second: Will Mitcham (U2 Mk2)
Third: Christopher Drake (Terrier Mk 4 Series 1)

Race 16: **Historic Touring Car Challenge with Tony Dron Trophy**

First: Harry & Nick Whale (BMW M3 E30)
Second: Mark Smith/Arran Moulton-Smith (BMW M3 E30)
Third: Neil Brown/Richard Dutton (Ford Lotus Co ina)

Race 17: **FIA Masters Historic Formula One**

First: Nick Padmore (Williams FW07C)
Second: Michael Lyons (Hesketh 308E)
Third: Christophe D'Ansembourg (Williams FW07C)

Race 18: **JET Super Touring Car Trophy**

First: James Dodd (Honda Accord)
Second: Rickard Rydell (Volvo S40)
Third: John Cleland (Vauxhall Vectra)

Race 19: **Masters Endurance Legends**

First: Steve Tandy (Lola B12/60)
Second: Hervé Regout (Lola Aston DBR1-2)
Third: David Porter (Peugeot 908)

Race 20: **Adrian Flux Trophy for pre 1966 Grand Prix Cars**

First: Peter Horsman (Lotus 18/21)
Second: Mark Daniell (Cooper T45)
Third: Tony Wood (Maserati Tec Mec)

Race 21: **Transatlantic Trophy for pre 1966 Touring Cars**

First: Mike Gardiner/Andy Wolfe (Ford Falcon)
Second: Craig Davies(Ford Mustang)
Third: James Thorpe/Sean McInerney (Ford Mustang)

First lap of the Gallett Trophy for Pre-1966 Grand Prix Cars. Barry Cannell, Brabham BT11A (#3), and Jon Farley, Brabham BT11/19 (#11) lead this gaggle of mid-field runners through Copse. Visible through the exhaust haze are the Scarab Offenhauser of Julian Bronson (#30) and the Lotus 18 373 driven by Benn Tilley (#69).

SILVERSTONE CLASSIC 2019

July 26th. – July 28th.

After the scorching weather enjoyed at 2018's Classic, and with the same at 2019's Friday qualifying, Saturday's early morning rain was a disappointment. Even though the rain relented later, only to return on Sunday morning, the weekend was generally dull, grey, windy and a touch on the chilly side.

This, however, didn't seem to dampen the enthusiasm of the large crowds that turned out on both days to witness this now famous festival of historic racing, with the organisers reporting yet another record-breaking year.

Over the three days, visitors were treated to a packed 21 race schedule ranging from Historic Formula 3 to the Sir Jackie Stewart Trophy race for FIA Masters Historic F1. Other races were for Historic F2, pre-'56 and pre-'61 Sportscars, Thundersports, pre-'63 GT cars, pre'66 GP Cars, pre-'66 Touring Cars, pre-War Sports Cars, Historic Sports Cars, Masters Endurance Legends Classic GT Cars (pre-'66) — plus, celebrating its 60th Anniversary, a massive 57-car grid of Minis.

In addition to all the on-track motorsport action, enthusiasts could mix with the teams and drivers in the garages in both the National and International Paddocks (as well as enjoying the myriad of attractions available for petrolheads and non-petrolheads alike.

We couldn't make it to Friday qualifying; but were there for the first race on Saturday, for HSCC Classic Formula 3 cars. On a wet track Dane Christian Olsen (1994 Martini Mk39) led the pack home by over four seconds from Ian Jacobs' 1984 Ralt RT3. The pair finished in the same order in Sunday's race with Christian increasing his winning margin to 16 seconds.

Still raining for the second race of the day, the RAC Woodcote Trophy for pre-1956 Sportscars & Stirling Moss Trophy for pre-1961 Sportscars. Oliver Bryant (1958 Lotus 15) and David Hart (1959 Lister Costin) swapped places a number of times in their battle for the lead before Bryant eventually brought the Lotus home in first place, while the Pearson brothers' 1955 Jaguar D-Type bagged the Woodcote Trophy.

The HSCC Thundersports race saw the awesome 1972 McLaren M8F with Dean Forward at the helm (quite apt given the conditions) get the better of Georg Hallau in the Lola T310 to take the win on a track better suited to powerboats than CanAm cars. In Sunday's running of the Thundersports race Hallau took the honours while mechanical problems forced Forward to retire.

Saturday's Formula 2 winner, Miles Griffiths (1978 Ralt RT1) had to settle for second on Sunday, behind Martin O'Connell (1977 Chevron B40) who took the flag despite a last lap spin.

The Tourist Trophy race for Historic (pre-1963) GT Cars brought Saturday morning's proceedings to a close with a win for the raucous bare-metal AC Cobra piloted by Martin Hunt who fended of the Jaguar E-Type of James Cottingham and Harvey Stanley, with the Ferrari 250 GT 'Breadvan' of Lukas and Niklas Halusa claiming third place in the last moments of the race.

Racing recommenced after the Saturday lunch break with the Jackie Stewart Trophy race for FIA Masters F1, in which Matteo Ferrer-Aza (1979 Ligier JS11/15) mastered a still wet track to score a convincing win by almost six seconds over Martin Stretton's 1983 Tyrrell 012. Sunday's running of the same race saw Steve Hartley in the ex-John Watson McLaren MP4/1 beat the Williams FW07C of Mike Cantillon to the flag by just 0.382 seconds.

F1 fans had a special treat with the appearance on track of Jackie Stewart. The three times World Champion climbed into the Matra MS80-02 in which he won his first World Championship in 1969 and, to the cheers of the crowd (and marshals) completed a number of demonstration laps. Not bad for an 80 year old!

Stewart was present, not just to celebrate the fiftieth anniversary of his first British GP win at Silverstone in 1969, but also to help raise awareness of his charity *Race Against Dementia* to which the Silverstone Classic's official Charity Partner, Alzheimer's Research UK donated all funds raised over the weekend.

The first of two Mini Celebration races saw a huge 57-car grid (including a 'Woody' estate variant) take to the track on Saturday afternoon in which victory went to Darren Turner by just 0.74s over Chris Middlehurst. Fittingly, on the 60th anniversary of the Mini, the final race of the weekend was the second Mini Celebration Trophy in which the victory went to current BTCC driver Adam Morgan over Ian Curley.

Will Nuthall in a 1960 Cooper T53 beat Sam Wilson (1960 Lotus 18) to the finish line in Saturday's running of the Gallet Trophy for pre-1969 GP Cars, while on Sunday Sam Wilson took the honours from Jon Fairley (Brabham BT11).

The Transatlantic Trophy for pre-1966 Touring Cars saw an epic struggle for the lead between the Rob Fenn/Jake Hill Ford Mustang and the similar car of Craig Davies which was interrupted when they made contact forcing Hill to spin. Davies let Hill back into the lead; but collision damage caused bodywork to rub on Hill's left rear tyre which led to a blow-out on the final lap. Hill made it to the chequered flag on three wheels thanks to Davies' generosity in not passing for the rest of the lap.

Staying with the saloon car theme, the Historic Touring Car Challenge for cars from 1966-1990, saw Michael Lyons cruise to a well-earned victory in his Spa 24-Hours winning Ford Sierra Cosworth RS500, with Craig Davies (also in a Sierra Cosworth) stealing second on the final corner from Steve Dance's Capri.

In July 1919 WO Bentley founded his eponymous company and, fittingly, the Bentley Centenary Trophy race for pre-War Sports Cars was won by the father/son team of Tim and Oliver Llewellyn driving an 8-litre Bentley 8/3 from 1926, after beating off the challenge from Rüdiger Friedrichs' 1933 Alvis Firefly.

Coming further up to date in Le Mans history the Yokohama Trophy for FIA Master Historic Sports Cars saw the Banks brothers, Andrew and Max, take the victory in their 1968 McLaren M6B from Gary Pearson's 1969 Lola T70.

The last race on Saturday evening evoked memories of more recent Le Mans 24 hour races with the 180+ mph prototypes hurtling into the gathering twilight. The Pescarolo LMP1 of Mike Cantillon/Jonathan Kennard headed the field at the flag, followed by the 2012 Lola B12 driven by Steve Tandy, and the same combination of cars/drivers finished Sunday's race in the same order. For most spectators, however, the main interest was probably the UK racing debut of the Bentley Speed 8 (the car that gave Bentley its most recent win at Le Mans in 2003.

PJO

Jackie Stewart at the wheel of his 1969 F1 World Championship winning Matra.

2019

A divers suit, rather than a fireproof suit, might have been a better choice for Georg Hallau judging by the amount of water rolling over his Lola T310 during Saturday's very wet HSCC Thundersports sprint race.

Perhaps the longest and widest CanAm car ever, the single T310 produced by Lola for Carl Haas' 1972 campaign suffered from too little development and testing with the result that driver David Hobb's highest finish was fourth at Watkins Glen when the front-running Porsches retired.

Katsuaki Kubota in the Lotus 91/7 (#2) splashes through the atrocious conditions for Sunday's F1 race ahead of Mark Hazell's Williams FW08C (#16), Antoine D'Ansembourg in the Brabham BT49 (#47), and the March 761 of Henry Fletcher (#34).

The Lotus 91 was the second F1 car manufactured from carbon fibre and Kevlar to race, after the McLaren MP4. Although the earlier Lotus 88 was also manufactured from the same composite materials, its ingenious twin chassis construction was deemed illegal by the FIA and although driven in practice for the 1981 US Grand Prix West at Long Beach by Elio de Angelis it never actually raced,

2019

2019

Italian driver Matteo Ferrer-Aza (1979 Ligier JS11/15) mastered the wet track on Saturday to score a convincing win by almost six seconds over Martin Stretton's 1983 Tyrrell 012.

Driven by Jacques Lafitte the JS11 won the first two races of the 1979 F1 season; but, while in contention throughout the year, the team finished third in the Constructor's Championship behind Ferrari and Williams, with Lafitte taking fourth spot in the Driver's Championship.

Michiel Campagne qualified this March 717 on the fifth row of the grid for Saturday's Thundersports sprint race, but finished towards the back of the field. He did better in Sunday's longer race, finishing in 12th.

The success of the North American Can-Am Challenge Cup for Group 7 cars spawned the European 'Interserie' championship for both Group 7 and Group 5 cars in 1970. Aiming for success in both championships March introduced the 707, designed by Robin Herd, which featured an unusual 'Hammerhead Shark' nose similar to the March 701 Formula One car. The first 707 was sold to German driver Helmut Kelleners who won two Interserie races in 1970 at Croft and Hockenheim.

March's ambitious programme of producing cars for Formula Ford, F2, F3, and F1 caused delays in building a second 707 for Chris Amon to race in Can-Am, prompting Amon to bring his long-time racing mechanic, fellow New Zealander Bruce Wilson, in to help speed up the process. However the car only appeared for the last three races of the 1970 Can-Am season, with Amon qualifying in third and finishing fifth on the car's first outing at Donnybrooke, Minnesota. In the last two races, at Laguna Seca and Riverside, Amon brought the 707 home in fourth place.

At the end of 1970 both cars were returned to the March factory in Bicester and uprated to 717 specification including a more conventional front end as seen here. Kelleners' car returned to the 1971 Interserie; but reliability problems meant his only finish in the top nine was at Keimola in Finland where he took the last podium spot from second on the grid.

After the promising end to the 1970 season the March works team did not return to Can-Am for the 1971 season, concentrating on their single-seater car production.

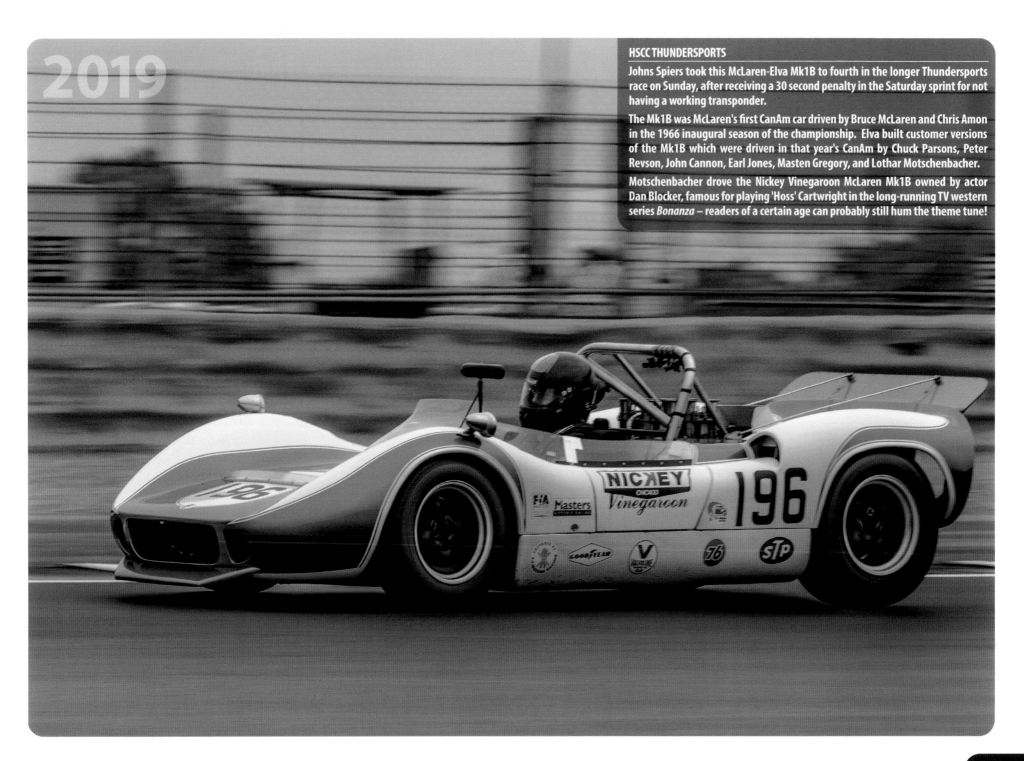

2019

HSCC THUNDERSPORTS

Johns Spiers took this McLaren-Elva Mk1B to fourth in the longer Thundersports race on Sunday, after receiving a 30 second penalty in the Saturday sprint for not having a working transponder.

The Mk1B was McLaren's first CanAm car driven by Bruce McLaren and Chris Amon in the 1966 inaugural season of the championship. Elva built customer versions of the Mk1B which were driven in that year's CanAm by Chuck Parsons, Peter Revson, John Cannon, Earl Jones, Masten Gregory, and Lothar Motschenbacher.

Motschenbacher drove the Nickey Vinegaroon McLaren Mk1B owned by actor Dan Blocker, famous for playing 'Hoss' Cartwright in the long-running TV western series *Bonanza* – readers of a certain age can probably still hum the theme tune!

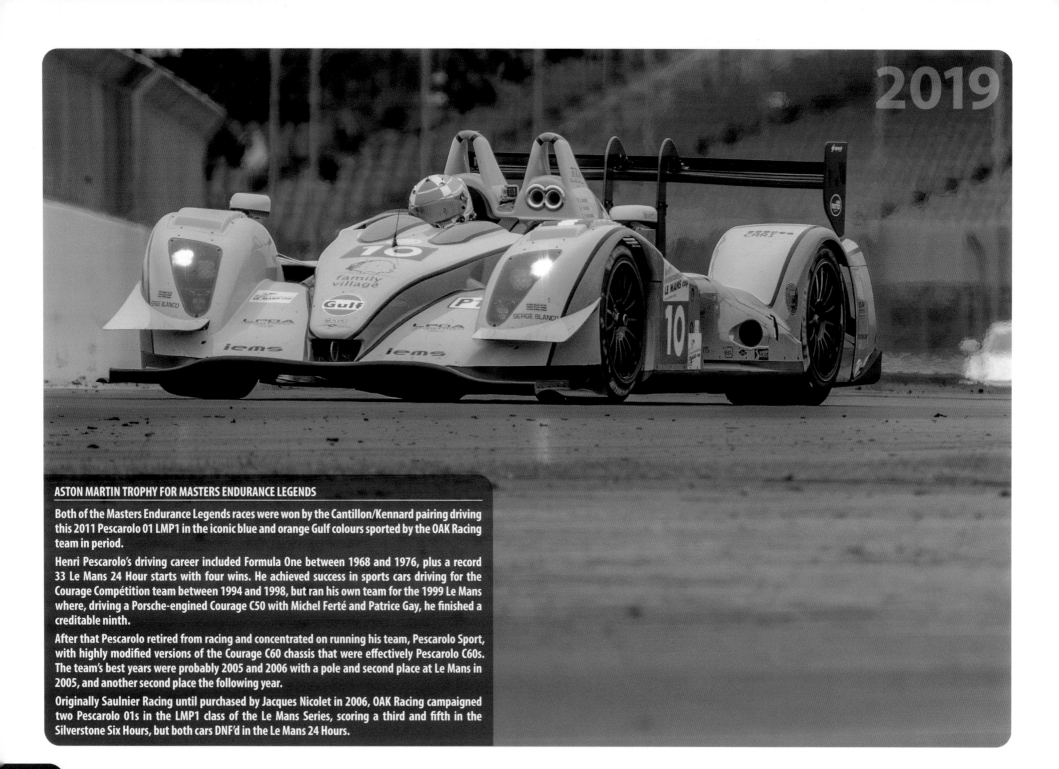

ASTON MARTIN TROPHY FOR MASTERS ENDURANCE LEGENDS

Both of the Masters Endurance Legends races were won by the Cantillon/Kennard pairing driving this 2011 Pescarolo 01 LMP1 in the iconic blue and orange Gulf colours sported by the OAK Racing team in period.

Henri Pescarolo's driving career included Formula One between 1968 and 1976, plus a record 33 Le Mans 24 Hour starts with four wins. He achieved success in sports cars driving for the Courage Compétition team between 1994 and 1998, but ran his own team for the 1999 Le Mans where, driving a Porsche-engined Courage C50 with Michel Ferté and Patrice Gay, he finished a creditable ninth.

After that Pescarolo retired from racing and concentrated on running his team, Pescarolo Sport, with highly modified versions of the Courage C60 chassis that were effectively Pescarolo C60s. The team's best years were probably 2005 and 2006 with a pole and second place at Le Mans in 2005, and another second place the following year.

Originally Saulnier Racing until purchased by Jacques Nicolet in 2006, OAK Racing campaigned two Pescarolo 01s in the LMP1 class of the Le Mans Series, scoring a third and fifth in the Silverstone Six Hours, but both cars DNF'd in the Le Mans 24 Hours.

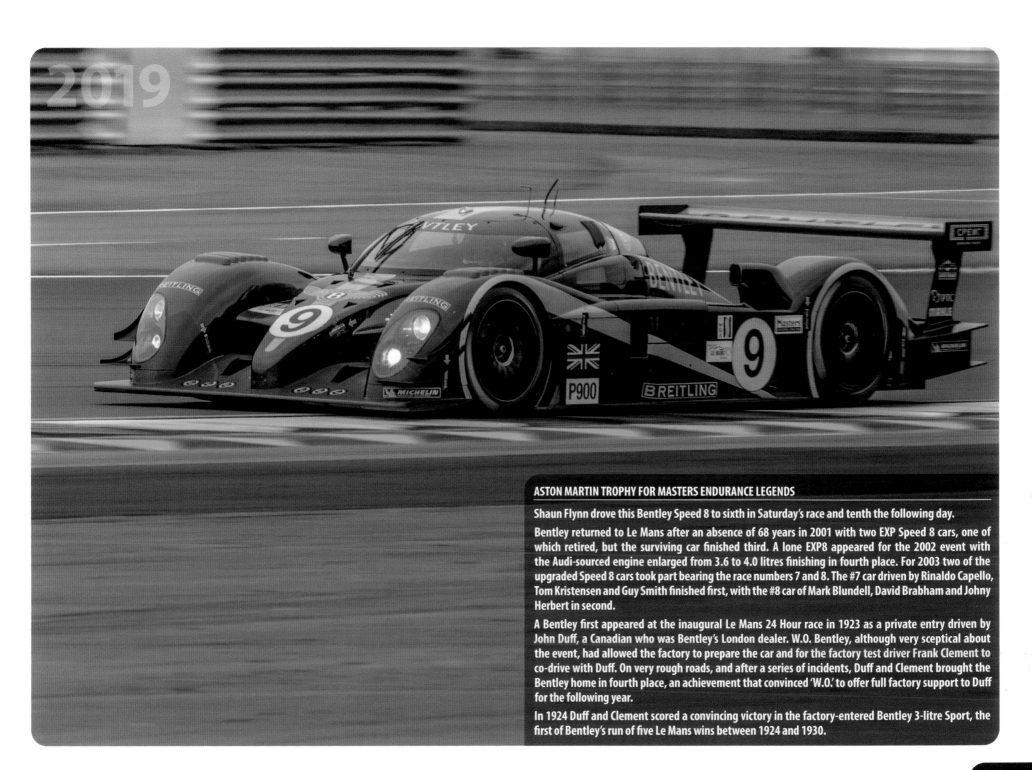

ASTON MARTIN TROPHY FOR MASTERS ENDURANCE LEGENDS

Shaun Flynn drove this Bentley Speed 8 to sixth in Saturday's race and tenth the following day.

Bentley returned to Le Mans after an absence of 68 years in 2001 with two EXP Speed 8 cars, one of which retired, but the surviving car finished third. A lone EXP8 appeared for the 2002 event with the Audi-sourced engine enlarged from 3.6 to 4.0 litres finishing in fourth place. For 2003 two of the upgraded Speed 8 cars took part bearing the race numbers 7 and 8. The #7 car driven by Rinaldo Capello, Tom Kristensen and Guy Smith finished first, with the #8 car of Mark Blundell, David Brabham and Johny Herbert in second.

A Bentley first appeared at the inaugural Le Mans 24 Hour race in 1923 as a private entry driven by John Duff, a Canadian who was Bentley's London dealer. W.O. Bentley, although very sceptical about the event, had allowed the factory to prepare the car and for the factory test driver Frank Clement to co-drive with Duff. On very rough roads, and after a series of incidents, Duff and Clement brought the Bentley home in fourth place, an achievement that convinced 'W.O.' to offer full factory support to Duff for the following year.

In 1924 Duff and Clement scored a convincing victory in the factory-entered Bentley 3-litre Sport, the first of Bentley's run of five Le Mans wins between 1924 and 1930.

GALLET TROPHY FOR PRE-1966 GP CARS

Tony Wood gets the front offside wheel airborne in the Maserati Tec-Mec around Copse corner.

In 1958 former Maserati designer Valerio Colotti founded Tec-Mec (Studio Tecnica Meccanica) to build a new Formula One car.

Based on the Maserati 250F, which Colotti had also designed, the Tec-Mec made its race debut at the 1959 US Grand Prix driven by Fritz d'Orey who qualified 17th on the grid but retired after six laps with an oil leak. This was the car's only Formula One outing.

GALLET TROPHY FOR PRE-1966 GP CARS

Will Nuthall in this Cooper T53 (#10) took the win in Saturday's running of the Gallet Trophy with Sam Wilson in a Lotus 18 in second spot. Wilson, whose green and purple helmet is just visible behind Nuthall, triumphed in Sunday's race.

The Cooper T53 was the most successful car in the 1960 Formula One season, with Bruce McLaren winning the opening round in Argentina and Jack Brabham first in five consecutive races to take his second driver's title and Cooper taking their second constructor's championship

INTERNATIONAL TROPHY FOR PRE-1966 CLASSIC GT CARS

Paul Pochciol and James Hansen drove this Shelby Daytona Cobra in the colours of Ecurie Ford France as raced at the 1965 1000km of Nürburgring by Jo Schlesser and Andre Simon.

Carroll Shelby realised that the open-cockpit roadster Cobra did not have the straight line speed to compete with the more aerodynamic Ferrari 250GTO along the Mulsanne straight at Le Mans. He asked Pete Brock, then an employee, to design a car that would overcome that disadvantage.

The resulting coupé made its race debut at the Daytona 200 Kilometres race on February 16 1964, where Dave MacDonald put the car on pole and set fastest lap during the race only to be eliminated after 202 laps with a fire.

The original six Daytona Coupés were entered by Alan Mann Racing (AMR) in many endurance races through 1964 and 1965, including the 1964 Le Mans 24 Hours where the Dan Gurney and Bob Bondurant driven car won the GT3 class and finished fourth overall.

INTERNATIONAL TROPHY FOR PRE-1966 CLASSIC GT CARS

Aston Martin built just two of these DP214 cars for the 1963 Le Mans 24 Hours to be driven by the driver pairings of Bruce McLaren/Innes Ireland and Jo Schlesser/Bill Kimberley. Both cars suffered piston failure leading to their retirements. Aston Martin sold the cars at the end of the 1963 season and in 1964 Mike Salmon earned the best DP124 finish with second place at the Silverstone International Trophy. The other DP214 was destroyed in a fatal crash during practice for the 1964 Nürburgring 1000 km race.

This DP214, one of three recreations, is owned by Aston Martin collector and racer Wolfgang Friedrichs who, with Simon Hadfield, took the car to a respectable finish in the International Trophy.

HISTORIC TOURING CAR CHALLENGE

Michael Lyons qualified this Ford Sierra Cosworth RS500 on pole and finished in first place 10 seconds in front of second place man Craig Davies in another Sierra RS500.

Homologated in August 1987, the new RS500 dominated the rest of that year's WTCC, with pole positions at all of the remaining races and clinching wins in four of them for the works-backed Eggenberger Motorsport team

Gianfranco Brancatelli, Bernd Schneider and Win Percy were the winning drivers of the Bastos-sponsored Sierra RS500 at the 1989 Spa S4 Hours, with the second Bastos Racing Team RS500 piloted by Frank Biela, Eddie Joosen and Thomas Lindstrom finishing in third.

HISTORIC TOURING CAR CHALLENGE

David Tomlin took this Zakspeed Escort RS1800 to sixth place in the Historic Touring Car Challenge.

Ford's official team in the 1976 Deutsch Rennsport Meisterschaft (DRM), the forerunner of the current DTM, was Zakspeed who entered two RS1800s driven by Hans Heyer and Klaus Ludwig, with Heyer taking the championship win from Ludwig in second place.

BENTLEY CENTENARY TROPHY FOR PRE-WAR SPORTS CARS

The 1931 Invicta S-Type Low Chassis driven by Chris and Nick Ball passes the 1934 Aston Martin Ulster driven by Holly Mason-Franchitti (daughter of Pink Floyd drummer Nick Mason, and wife of 2014 Sebring 12 Hours winner Marino Franchitti) and James Wood.

"The low chassis Invicta was probably the best-looking sports car in the vintage tradition ever to be produced in England. I can think of no contemporary unsupercharged motor-car of similar capacity, made here, which could outperform it - and very few built elsewhere..." (J R Buckley, 'The 4½-litre S-Type Invicta', Profile Publications, 1966).

The Invicta S Type was successful in long distance trials of the time including winning the 1931 Monte Carlo Rally driven by Donald Healey.

BENTLEY CENTENARY TROPHY FOR PRE-WAR SPORTS CARS

Pit stops are a feature of Silverstone Classic races in which drivers share cars, while lone drivers also have to stop for a designated time period. Here Richard Bradley in the red Aston Martin Ulster waits for the mandatory 15 seconds to elapse before departing the International Pits. In the background Gregor Fisken jumps aboard the Vauxhall 30/98 while co-driver Jeremy Brewster holds the door open.

BENTLEY CENTENARY TROPHY FOR PRE-WAR SPORTS CARS

Tim Llewellyn at the wheel of this 1926 Bentley 3/8 before handing over to his son Oliver on the way to first place in Saturday's Bentley Centenary Trophy for Pre-War Sports Cars.

The Bentley has been in the Llewellyn family since the late 1950s when Tim's father bought the car in a sad state and also fitted with a saloon body. After rebuilding the car he raced it with a 6.5 litre engine between 1963 and 1968, after which it was fitted with its current 8-litre power unit. Tim has driven it since the 1980s.

BENTLEY CENTENARY TROPHY FOR PRE-WAR SPORTS CARS

Bentley Boys! Martin Overington in the 1929 4.5 litre 'Blower' Bentley (#2) alongside the 1922 Bentley 3/4.5 (#48) driven by Randal Stewart and William Elbourn through Club corner.

The 'Blower' Bentley was the brainchild of Sir Henry 'Tim' Birkin who, sharing a 6.6 litre Bentley Speed Six with Bentley Chairman Woolf Barnato, won the 1929 Le Mans 24 Hours leading three 4.5 litre Bentleys home.

WO Bentley opposed Birkin's supercharger idea but, with financial backing from wealthy, eccentric racehorse owner Dorothy Paget, Birkin persuaded Barnato to approve the construction of 50 supercharged 4.5 litre Bentleys to meet the homologation requirements of the Automobile Club de l'Ouest in order to compete at the 1930 Le Mans.

The two privateer 'Blower' Bentleys were fast with the Birkin /Jean Chassagne car battling for the lead with the Mercedes of Rudolph Caracciola/Christian Werner in the early stages. However, tyre problems delayed them and after 138 laps the engine blew. The second 'Blower' car of Dudley Benjafield and Giulio Ramponi retired a few laps later with the same problem, leaving the win to the more reliable Speed Six Bentley of Barnato and Glen Kidston.

RACE RESULTS Silverstone Classic 2019

Race 1: **HSCC Classic Formula 3**
First: Christian Olsen (Martini MK39)
Second: Ian Jacobs (Ralt RT3)
Third: Andrew Smith (March 783)

Race 2: **Royal Automobile Club Woodcote and Stirling Moss Trophy**
First: Oliver Bryant (Lotus 15)
Second: David Hart (Lister Costin)
Third: Tony Wood/Will Nuthall (Lister Knobbly)

Race 3: **HSCC Thundersports**
First: Dean Forward (McLaren M8F)
Second: Georg Hallau (Lola T310)
Third: Robert Beebee (Lola T70 Mk3B)

Race 4: **HSCC Historic Formula 2**
First: Miles Griffiths (Ralt RT1)
Second: Darwin Smith (March 722)
Third: Andy Smith (March 722)

Race 5: **Royal Automobile Club Tourist Trophy for Historic Cars (Pre 1963 GT)**
First: Patrick Blakeney-Edwards/Martin Hunt (AC Cobra)
Second: James Cottingham/Harvey Stanley (Jaguar E-Type)
Third: Niklas Halusa/Lukas Halusa (Ferrari 250 GT 'Breadvan')

Race 6: **Sir Jackie Stewart Trophy for FIA Masters Historic Formula One**
First: Matteo Ferrer-Aza (Ligier JS11/15)
Second: Martin Stretton (Tyrrell 012)
Third: Mike Cantillon (Williams FW07C)

Race 7: **Mini Celebration Trophy presented by Adrian Flux**
First: Darren Turner (Austin Mini Cooper S)
Second: Chris Middlehurst (Morris Mini Cooper S)
Third: Adam Morgan (Morris Mini Cooper S)

Race 8: **Gallet Trophy for Pre 1966 Grand Prix Cars**
First: Will Nuthall (Cooper T53)
Second: Sam Wilson (Lotus 16 368)
Third: Michael Griffiths (Cooper T79)

Race 9: **Transatlantic Trophy for Pre 1966 Touring Cars**
First: Rob Fenn/Jake Hill (Ford Mustang)
Second: Craig Davies (Ford Mustang)
Third: Andy Wolfe (Ford Lotus Cortina)

Race 10: **Bentley Centenary Trophy for Pre-War Sports Cars**
First: Oliver Llewllyn/Tim Llewellyn (Bentley 3/8)
Second: Rüdiger Friedrichs (Alvis Firefly)
Third: Fred Wakeman/Patrick Blakeney-Edwards (Frazer Nash Super Sports)

Race 11: **Yokohama Trophy for FIA Masters Historic Sports Cars**
First: Andrew Banks/Max Banks (McLaren M6B)
Second: Gary Pearson (Lola T70 MK3B)
Third: Diogo Ferrao (Lola T292)

Race 12: **Aston Martin Trophy for Masters Endurance Legends**
First: Mike Cantillon/Jonathan Kennard (Pescarolo LMP1)
Second: Steve Tandy (Lola B12/60)
Third: Christophe D'Ansembourg (Lola Aston Martin DBR1-2)

Race 13: **HSCC Classic F3**
First: Christian Olsen (Martini MK39))
Second: Ian Jacobs (Ralt RT3)
Third: Adrian Langridge (March 803)

Race 14: HSCC Thundersports Endurance
First: Georg Hallau (Lola T310
Second: John Burton (Chevron B26)
Third: Robert Beebee/Joshua Beebee (Lola T70 Mk3B)

Race 15: HSCC Historic Formula 2
First: Martin O'Connell (Chevron B40)
Second: Miles Griffiths (Ralt RT1)
Third: Darwin Smith (March 722)

Race 16: Historic Touring Car Challenge
First: Michael Lyons (Ford Sierra Cosworth RS500)
Second: Craig Davies (Ford Sierra Cosworth RS500)
Third: Steve Dance (Ford Capri)

Race 17: Sir Jackie Stewart Trophy for FIA Masters Historic Formula One
First: Steve Hartley (McLaren MP4/1)
Second: Mike Cantillon (Williams FW07C)
Third: Christophe D'Ansembourg (Williams FW07C)

Race 18: International Trophy for Classic GT Cars (Pre 1966)
First: Julian Thomas/Callum Lockie (Shelby Daytona Cobra)
Second: David Hart/ Oliver Hart (AC Cobra Daytona Coupe)
Third: Graeme Dodd/James Dodd (Jaguar E-Type)

Race 19: Gallet Trophy for Pre 1966 Grand Prix Cars (HGPCA)
First: Sam Wilson (Lotus 18 372)
Second: Jon Fairley (Brabham BT11/19)
Third: Will Nuthall (Cooper T53) +6.315s

Race 20: Aston Martin Trophy for Masters Endurance Legends
First: Mike Cantillon/Jonathan Kennard (Pescarolo LMP1)
Second: Steve Tandy (Lola B12/60)
Third: David Porter (Peugeot 90X)

Race 2 Mini Celebration Trophy Presented By Adrian Flux
First: Adam Morgan (Morris Mini Cooper S)
Second: Ian Curley (Austin Mini Cooper S)
Third: Michael Caine (Austin Mini Cooper S)

RACE 20: ASTON MARTIN TROPHY FOR MASTERS ENDURANCE LEGENDS

The Simon Watts/Roberto Giordanelli Lola B2K/40 streaks around Copse corner.

Splashing through Abbey in the rain during the 60th Anniversary E-Type Challenge are the Jaguar E-Types of Rick Willmott (#84), Gary Pearson (#23), Dodd/Dodd (#21), and Fisher/Owens (#60).

The Silverstone Classic, re-branded as Classic Silverstone, returned over the last weekend of July, after the COVID-enforced cancellation of the 2020 event, bigger and better than ever, even though the weather threatened to spoil the fun with a number of races interrupted by heavy rain.

Kicking off proceedings on Saturday morning was the first of two races for Historic Formula Junior cars. On a slightly damp track pole sitter Cameron Jackson in a Brabham BT2 led a breakaway group of Richard Bradley in a similar car and Pierre Livingston until Livingston spun at Brooklands on lap three. Jackson and Bradley then diced for the lead until Bradley managed to get past while lapping slower cars at Club and held on to win by 1.8 seconds.

Next up was the Motor Racing Legends 'BRDC 500' race for Pre-War sports cars in which pole sitter Fred Wakeman took his chain-driven Frazer-Nash TT replica in to a storming lead from the off, which second driver Pat Blakeney-Edwards maintained for the last ten minutes to the flag. Sue Darbyshire managed third spot on the grid in Friday's wet qualifying in the (also chain-driven) Morgan Super Aero; but Saturday's dry track didn't favour her and she finished in 11th.

Saturday's third race, for Historic Formula 2, saw pole sitter Matthew Wrigley (1978 March 782) get away cleanly followed from third on the grid by Andrew Smith (1974 March 742) only for the Safety Car to be deployed before the field had finished the first lap as a tangle of cars resulted in one stuck in the gravel at Abbey. After the green flag Wrigley and Smith, joined later by Mark Griffiths, put on a superb display until a few laps from the end when Smith ran wide at Luffield letting Griffiths through although Smith got past again to claim second spot at the end. Unfortunately the race was red-flagged with one lap left to go when Rob Wainwright's spin in the Crossle 22F at Club left the car in a dangerous position.

The Historic Tourist Trophy race saw Nigel Greensall (Jaguar E-Type) take an early lead from 5th on the grid from the similar E-Types of James Cottingham and Jack Minshaw who later beached the car after spinning out on oil laid down by the Van Lanschott/ Le Blanc Austin Healey 3000 on the approach to Abbey. Martin Brundle had taken the E-Type shared with Garry Pearson temporarily into the lead of the race before retiring. After the resulting long safety car period to remove Minshaw's car and clean up the oil slick, Lucas Halusa got the Ferrari 250GT 'Breadvan' in front of the Jaguars to take the win from the Cottingham/Stanley E-Type.

The Master Historic Formula 1 race featured a Tyrrell driven by Ken Tyrrell, no obviously not THAT Ken Tyrrell, this Ken Tyrrell is an American driver who decided if he was going to drive any F1 car it just had to be a Tyrrell, so he bought the car with which Michele Alboreto secured Tyrrell's penultimate victory at Las Vegas in 1982 and qualified it ninth on the grid for this race.

It was Michael Lyons in the Ensign N180B who dominated this race with an outstanding pole-to-flag win. Steve Hartley (McLaren MP4/1) spun out from third place at the end of lap one on the oil slick from the previous race at Abbey. Quickly recovering from that spin Hartley fought his way back to third in front of Steve Brooks in a Lotus 91 only to spin again at Becketts with Brooks clipping Hartley's front wheel as he took

avoiding action (luckily with no serious damage to either car.

The weather took a turn for the worse at the start of the Thundersports race which started on a dry track but with rain beginning to fall almost as soon as the lights went green. With heavy rain falling and the cars all on slicks, Dean Forward in the McLaren M8F CanAm car had an almighty spin at Farm before the race was red-flagged with just half a lap completed.

Organised chaos in pits as cars change to wets after red flag

After a delay to change to wets, the field was out again and the race re-started with Callum Lockie taking the March 717 into an immediate lead from Dean Forward, harried by the smaller cars of Ed Thurston (Chevron B19) and Tony Sinclair (Lola T292).

On a track still damp in places the two mighty CanAm cars of Lockie and Forward built a lead over the rest of the field until, with rain falling again, Forward lost the McLaren at Brooklands and spun off clouting the barrier with the right rear causing enough damage for him to head to the pits and retirement.

After a safety car to recover Peter Halford's damaged Corvette, and with all drivers having done their compulsory pit stop under the safety car, the race leader was Tony Sinclair with Callum Lockie way back in seventh. The last few laps saw a dramatic charge by Lockie through the field; but he narrowly failed to take Sinclair, losing out by just 3/10 second.

Drama at the start of the Mini Challenge when Ian Curley collided with Michael Collins through Farm Curve on lap one, which allowed Nathan Heathcote and Bill Sollis to open

Bill Sollis leads Mini train along damp Hamilton Straight

a gap between them and the chasing pack. On a damp but drying track a four car train led by Bill Sollis, with Heathcote, Chris Middlehurst and Endaf Owens slipped and slid around to finish in that order with Sollis taking the flag by 0.792 second.

Rüdiger Friedrichs (Cooper T53) took the lead from pole sitter Sam Wilson (Lotus 18) at Farm in the Pre-1966 Grand Prix cars race, albeit only temporarily as Wilson had it back by Brooklands. Wilson was in command of the race from then with Will Nuthall in another Cooper closing in the final laps but Wilson held on to win by 0.3 sec. Andrew Haddon in the front-engined Scarab-Offenhauser finished fourth despite having to start from the pit lane after the car was reluctant to start in the assembly area.

The Pre-1966 Touring Cars are always good to watch and this race was no exception. A damp (in parts) track narrowed the speed advantage of the USA heavy metal Ford Falcons and Mustangs (enlivened this year by the addition of a Studebaker Lark Daytona) over the more agile Lotus Cortinas and Minis.

Pole sitter Dave Coyne led from the start in his Ford Mustang but Nigel Greensall got very sideways at The Loop, was hit by another car and left stationary in the middle of the track.

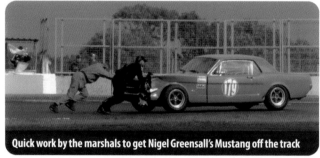

Quick work by the marshals to get Nigel Greensall's Mustang off the track

At the front, despite the best efforts of Richard Dutton in the Lotus Cortina, the big American V8s of Coyne, Julian Thomas (Ford Falcon) and Craig Davies (Ford Mustang) began to pull away, to be joined later by the Ford Falcon of Sam Tordoff who took the lead when Coyne drifted wide at Stowe. A gentle nudge from Coyne, now in third, sent Thomas spinning at Brooklands but he was able to rejoin albeit well down the field. A long pit stop with the bonnet up put paid to Tordoff's hopes of a win, and after everyone had made their stops the order at the front was Coyne, Davies, Dutton and Mark Farmer who had taken over the Studebaker from Adrian Wilmott.

A safety car with 10 minutes to run to recover a Mini in the gravel at Stowe allowed the Thomas Falcon, now with Callum Lockie behind the wheel, to catch up with the leaders. At the gravel at Stowe with major damage to both ends of the Falcon and a big dent to the front of Coyne's Mustang. At the flag Davies just held of Ben Clucas' Lotus Cortina with Steve Soper in the Alan Mann Racing liveried Mustang in third.

The Masters Endurance Legends race saw Rob Wheldon take the Lola to a fine win after battling with Francois Perrodo's Peugeot 908 for much of the race. With Perrodo classified as a 'Gentleman' driver and thus entitled to a shorter pit stop he gained a substantial lead after everyone had stopped; but Wheldon chased him down hard, repeatedly breaking the lap record in the process to take the victory by 4.8 seconds.

ADRIAN FLUX TROPHY FOR MRL HISTORIC TOURING CAR CHALLENGE

Mark Farmer and Adrian Willmott brought this ex-works Ford GA Capri home in eighth place, here ahead of the Ford RS500 driven by G and J Dodd.

Realising that no more horsepower could be extracted from the Weslake-modified 2.9 litre V6 Cologne engines that had powered the Capris in the 1972 European Touring Car Championship, Ford commissioned Cosworth to provide a new engine based on the 3.0 litre Essex engine. Radically different with twin overhead camshafts, alloy cylinder heads, 4 valves per cylinder and dry-sumped, the Cosworth GA engine produced over 460 bhp in race tune, enough to take the fight to BMW in 1974.

171

The Yokohama Trophy for Historic Sports Cars, started dry but was interrupted by rain which led to a number of 'offs' and brought out the safety car when the Chester/Ward Lola T70 got stuck in the gravel at Club, probably much to the chagrin of Alex Brundle who had built up a 15 second lead by that point. With torrential rain continuing (although it was dry at Copse!) the race was red-flagged. After the re-start Brundle controlled the shortened race to win from Oliver Bryant (Lola T70) and the Beighton/Hadfield Lola T70, although Tom Bradshaw in the pretty little Chevron B19 almost made it to a podium spot, just losing out by 0.7 second.

Saturday's final race, the RAC Woodcote and Stirling Moss Trophies race, was shortened to allowing finishing before the 9:00pm cut-off time and saw the Lister Knobbly of pole man Sam Hancock beaten away from the start by second spot driver Roger Wills in a Lotus 15. After yet another long safety car period to recover more cars, the Richard Bradley driven Lotus 15 was in front ahead of the Lister Knobbly of Ward/Smith. By the flag however Martin O'Connell in the diminutive Lotus 11 had stormed through the conditions to take the win by 7 seconds from Roger Wills' Lotus 15.

Formula Junior was again the first race on the Sunday morning and with the same duo battling for the lead, this time resolved in favour of Cameron Jackson who managed the slippery conditions to bring his Brabham BT2 home 2.5 seconds in front of Richard Bradley in his similar car. The last podium spot was taken by Pierre Livingston nearly 26 seconds behind Jackson.

Misty persistent rain posed visibility problems for both drivers and spectators during the Adrian Flux Trophy for MRL Historic Touring Cars, in which Paul Mensley's Ford Sierra Cosworth leaped into an early lead, followed in the gloom by Simon Garrard (Nissan Skyline R32) and pole sitter David Tomlin in a Sierra RS500.

After the compulsory pit stops the leader was Dave Coyne in the Sierra he'd taken over from Mark Wright with an almost 30 second advantage over the second placed man Mathew Ellis who'd replaced Mensley. It wasn't long however until Ellis retired the Sierra with mechanical problems, promoting Steve Dance's Ford Capri into second, followed by Garrad in the Nissan which seemed to have recovered from whatever problem had slowed it down for a few laps.

At the flag Coyne took the win by 51 seconds ahead of Steve Dance's Capri and the Sierra Cosworth driven by Steve Soper and Craig Davies. Garrard's Nissan had slipped down to fourth at the end. The Tony Dron Trophy section of the race was won by the Marcus Jewel/Ben Clucas Ford Capri from the VW Scirroco of Morris/Shepherd.

With rain continuing the Historic F2 cars came out to play. Initially this looked like a replay of Saturday's race just with added spray as Matthew Wrigley led from Andrew Smith, until on lap 4 Smith squeezed past going through the Loop and pulled out a controlling lead, winning at the flag by almost six seconds over Wrigley, with Mike Griffiths again bringing his Ralt home in third.

A full grid lined up for the 60th Anniversary E-Type Challenge, still under misty rain and leaden skies. Early leader Nigel Greensall, followed by Ben Mitchell until Mitchell found a way past Greensall on lap 4. Mitchell began to pull away from a battle for second between Greensall, Alex Brundle and Danny Winstanley, until Brundle began to drop back through the field looking as though he was suffering from lack of vision due to a misted screen and the loss of the driver's side wiper.

After the pit window had closed the Spiers/Needell car was shown on top of the leader board but they had not taken the mandatory pit stop so were excluded from the race. I'm thinking that Tiff was not best pleased with that as he didn't even get a turn behind the wheel of the E-Type.

When the car of Graham and Alan Bull ended up beached in the gravel at Becketts the race was red flagged on lap 10 and not re-started, leaving Mitchell as the first over the line followed by Winstanley and Gary Pearson — however some black magic sorcery elevated Jon Minshaw to the first spot over Mitchell, even though he was shown in sixth place on lap 9 and had also collected a 30 second time penalty for pitting outside of the pit window!

A reverse grid for the Masters Historic F1, based on finishing positions in Saturday's race, saw Lucas Halusa on pole in the McLaren M23 and the previous day's winner Michael Lyons fifth on the grid. While not raining hard as for the previous E-Type race, the track was still wet enough for the pace car to get a bit sideways at Luffield as they led the cars round! From fifth place the rapid Lyons took the lead at Stowe on the first lap and began to build a commanding lead which he held to the flag. Mike Cantillon (Williams FW07C) was 14.4 seconds behind with Steve Hartley (McLaren MP4/1) third.

Following Damon Hill's demo laps in his 1995 title-winning Williams the pre-1966 GP cars took to the rapidly drying track for their second race of the weekend. Unfortunately

MASTERS ENDURANCE LEGENDS

From right: The first, second and fourth place finishers in Masters Endurance Legends: Francois Perrodo (Peugeot 908), Shaun Lynn (Peugeot 908), Emmanuel Collard (Porsche RS Spyder)

Saturday's winner Sam Wilson didn't make the grid as his car was withdrawn. Rüdiger Freidrichs from second spot on the grid got the jump on pole man Will Nuthall to get in front by Abbey and led for most of the first lap, while Nuthall slowed and pitted with a problem. By lap two Andrew Haddon in the front-engined Scarab-Offenhauser had muscled himself to first spot where he stayed in a dominant performance to the flag, eight seconds in front of Freidrichs in second place.

The sun began to break through the clouds at last as the Classic GT cars came out for their race. Michael Cullen stormed through from eighth on the grid to lead the field into Abbey in his AC Cobra Daytona Coupé but lost out to the Julian Thomas and Oliver Bryant Cobras at Brooklands.

A nasty incident at Copse when a spinning Lotus Elan was collected by an unsighted Porsche left the Lotus with its front end destroyed and parked just off the track which resulted in a long safety car period to recover the car.

The threat of another safety car later, when the Joebst/Willis Lotus Elan rolled at Aintree, was averted when the driver managed to drive the car, now minus front and rear windows and passenger side door, to a place of safety (kudos to him after what looked to have been a really frightening incident.

Bryant's pit stop put him out alongside the Thomas/Lockie car, now in the hands of Callum Lockie, and Bryant muscled his way through as Lockie locked up on the way into Village, although the more aerodynamic Daytona Coupé of Lockie had the advantage down the Wellington Straight and took back the lead which he held to the finish.

The awesome Masters Endurance Legends cars saw Steve Tandy's Lola B12/60 lead from pole until Francois Perrodo's diesel-powered Peugot 908 blasted past down the Wellington Straight. Tandy faded away and a battle for the lead developed between the Peugeots of Perrodo and Shaun Lynn, with Lynn pulling away for top spot until Perrodo powered through with just over eight minutes to run and stayed there to the finish.

Concluding another fine weekend of racing at the Classic, the second running of the Mini Challenge started in bright sunshine unlike Saturday's wet race. Bill Sollis led from pole but ran wide at Club to let Nathan Heathcote through to be joined at the head of the field by Endaf Owens, and they finished in that order, with Bill Sollis in third. The final few laps were enlivened by a close battle for fourth between Jeff Smith, Aaron Smith and Chris Middlehurst with Jeff Smith taken fourth at the flag.

PJO

MURRAY WALKER MEMORIAL TROPHY FOR MASTERS HISTORIC FORMULA ONE

Ken Tyrrell (no, not THAT Ken Tyrrell) drove this Tyrrell 011 to ninth place in Race 1 and sixth in Race 2. Here he is ahead of Steve Brook in the JPS-liveried Lotus 91which finished last in Race 1 and fifth in Race 2.

Designed by Maurice Phillipe the Tyrrell 011 made its debut at the 1998 German GP in the hands of Eddie Cheever who finished in fifth. Two wins were scored by Michele Alboreto for Tyrrell, the 1982 Caesers Palace GP in Las Vegas and the 1983 Detroit GP, the latter the last GP win for the Ford Cosworth DFV engine after 16 years powering F1 cars to victory.

Richard Bradley (#81) and Cameron Jackson (#66), both in Brabham BT2s fought for the lead in both Saturday's and Sundays Formula junior races with Bradley coming out on top on Saturday and Jackson reversing the order on Sunday.

During the 1960s Motor Racing Developments, the company set up by Jack Brabham and Ron Tauranac, became the largest manufacturer of open-wheel racing cars with over 500 of its Brabham cars produced.

The BT2 was the first really successful series production model with 11 built in 1962, the first of which was bought by Briggs Cunningham who campaigned it in the USA. Other winning BT2 drivers in that year were Frank Gardner and Jo Schlesser.

HISTORIC FORMULA JUNIOR

Mid-field runners Robin Langdon, Lola Mk.5A (#5); James Hicks, Caravelle Mk.3 (#71); Nic Carlton-Smith, Keift FJ (#39) and Charlie Besley, Elva 100 (#114) round Luffield corner during Sunday's running of the Formula Junior race.

The pretty Caravelle series of Formula Junior cars were created by James' father Bob Hicks and Richard Utley, and Bob drove the Caravelles to some success in 1960/61 including a sixth place finish at the 1960 Oulton Park Gold Cup meeting.

Previously Bob Hicks had raced a Lotus Eleven extensively in Europe winning the Coupes d'Automne race at Montlhéry in 1957, and entering the 1958 Le Mans 24 Hours with Bill Frost as co-driver only to be eliminated in a crash during a torrential rainstorm after three hours.

MRL PRE WAR 'BRDC 500'

The tall Fred Wakeman towers above his Frazer Nash TT Replica that he co-drove with (the not quite so tall) Pat Blakeney-Edwards in a pole-to-flag win.

The TT Replica was the most numerous of the chain-driven Frazer Nash cars manufactured in the 1930s, and probably the most successful in competition, especially in the long-distance European reliability trials popular at the time.

TT Replicas are named after the 1931 Tourist Trophy race at the Ards circuit in Northern Ireland where three Frazer Nash cars were entered, although none of them finished. According to the September 1931 issue of *Motor Sport*, a little bit of fluff was the cause of one retirement with the magazine reporting: *"As we go to press the following telegram arrived from Mr. H. J. Aldington of Frazer-Nash Cars (A.F.N., Ltd.): — The joke is on us perfectly good motor car withdrawn officially with engine trouble discovered main jet one carburettor choked by fluff—Aldington."*

MRL PRE WAR 'BRDC 500'

A wet qualifying enabled Sue Darbyshire to place this 1929 Morgan Super Aero third on the grid. Drier race conditions however didn't favour the car so much and she finished eleventh, although second in the PW1 class.

Henry (HFS) Morgan founded his eponymous motor company in 1909 and the first Morgans were lightweight cyclecars (classed as motorcycles, so free of the tax on cars at the time), powered by V-Twin motorcycle engines from J.A.P., Matchless, Anzani or Blackburne mounted ahead of the front wheels and with a chain drive to the single rear wheel.

With their superior power-to weight ratio, Morgan three-wheelers were successful in motorsport with HFS Morgan himself winning the *Light Car and Cyclecar Challenge Trophy* at Brooklands in 1912. Many other successes followed including HFS setting the fastest cyclecar time at Kop Hill in 1924 and Morgan agent Harold Beart breaking the 100mph barrier for the first time in a three-wheeler at Brooklands in 1925.

Morgan's first four wheel car, the 4/4, was introduced in 1936, and at the 1938 24 Hours of Le Mans a 4/4 driven by Marjorie Fawcett and Geoffrey White finished in 13th place.

HSCC THUNDERSPORTS

Tony Sinclair drove this Lola T292 to first place in the Thundersports race.

Introduced in 1973, the T292 was an evolution from the highly successful T290, which claimed numerous significant victories including a class win at the 1972 Le Mans 24 Hours and a class win and fourth place overall in the Targa Florio the same year.

Immediately successful, the Crowne Racing T292, driven by Chris Craft, won five of the eight-round 1973 European 2-litre Championship giving Craft the Driver's title and Lola their second Manufacturer's Championship.

2021

HSCC THUNDERSPORTS

Julian Maynard at the wheel of the ex-Bobby Rahal Lola T290.

Bobby Rahal's father Michael purchased the Lola in 1973 and on the strength of his performances in the car Bobby earned himself a drive in the Canadian Formula Atlantic series in 1975, in which he finished second to Giles Villeneuve. The Lola was sold and subsequently campaigned in Can-Am and CASC events by new owners.

Rahal went on to a stellar career in CART winning 24 races, including the 1986 Indianapolis 500, and three championships in 1986, 1987, and 1992.

In 2001 Rahal tracked the Lola down, bought it back, restored it and raced it on a number of occasions including the Classic Endurance race at Silverstone in September 2009 where Rahal brought the Lola home first by five seconds from John Burton (*see page 216*) in his Chevron B26, after an epic battle between the two.

An unusual participant in that 2009 Silverstone race was a Bob McKee built Howmet TX gas turbine powered car driven by Xavier Micheron — which brings us on nicely to the car on the following page..

HSCC THUNDERSPORTS

Little is known about this McKee Mahyra before Greg Thornton bought the car, although it did come with a photo showing the car with a magnificent Trophy that the seller said proved it was a race winner (turned out the Trophy was for 'Custom Car of the Year 1963').

Bob McKee built a number of cars that competed in the US Road Racing Championship (USRRC), the precursor to the Can-Am series, during the early to mid-1960s although there appears to be no record of this car taking part. McKee also built the two Howmet TX gas turbine powered cars that competed at Le Mans in 1968. While both cars DNFd at Le Mans, two previous wins in the USA meant the Howmet was the first, and only, jet-powered car to have won races.

David 'Salt' Walther was an Indycar and NASCAR racer who survived an horrendous fiery crash in the 1973 Indianapolis 500; but again the author can find no evidence that he ever drove this car, or that he drove in any other series apart from Indycars or NASCAR.

Owner Thornton drove his car at The Classic to finish in 28th place.

2021

HSCC THUNDERSPORTS

A Lola T210 driven by Nick Pink splashes through the puddles exiting the International Pits on the way to a sixth place finish.

Lola designed the T210 to contest the new FIA European Championship for 2-litre sportscars in 1970. The car was competitive straight away, with Jo Bonnier winning a round of the British Sports Car Championship at Silverstone. Bonnier also won the closely fought European Championship drivers' title, although Chevron beat Lola to the manufacturer's title by just one point.

INTERNATIONAL TROPHY FOR CLASSIC GT CARS (Pre 1966)

The Ginetta G4R of Ron Maydon and Mike Wilds which finished a credible eighth behind much larger engined cars.

A Ginetta G4R bearing the race number 52 driven by American Jack Walsh who, with the Canadian pair Gordon Browne and Peter Keith, started the 1965 Sebring 12 Hour race but retired after 82 laps with engine trouble.

Mike Wilds' racing career includes a short, and less than stellar, stint in Formula One starting at the British GP in 1974. After failing to qualify for the 1976 British GP, he turned to other disciplines including the 1976 Shellsport International Formula Libre Series in which he finished fifth driving a Shadow DN3 and Ensign N174.

He has also driven eight times at Le Mans between 1981 and 1988, where his best result was 14th in 1988 driving a Nissan R88C shared with Alan Grice and Win Percy. In 2016 he finished eighth, and first in class, in the Britcar Endurance Championship driving a Ferrari 458 Challenge.

INTERNATIONAL TROPHY FOR CLASSIC GT CARS (Pre 1966)

Race winning Shelby Daytona Cobra (#192) of Thomas/Lockie leads second place AC Cobra driven by Oliver Bryant into Club Corner, ahead of Mike Whitaker's TVR Griffith (#46) which finished fourth.

Following are the Cullen/Shovlin AC Cobra Daytona (#69); James Cottingham's Shelby Cobra (#21) amd another Shelby Daytona Cobra driven by Hanson/Pochiol (#144). The tiny by comparison Ginetta of Ron Maydon and Mike Wilds lurks in the background.

Adrian Willmot and Mark Farmer drove this Studebaker Lark Daytona which made an unfamiliar addition to the big American V8s in the Transatlantic Trophy.

Struggling Studebaker was the first US car manufacturer to produce a "compact" car with the Lark which was introduced in 1959. Initially a sales success but the introduction of more competitively priced 'compact' cars by Ford, GM and Chrysler reduced sales to such an extent that Studebaker shut down their South Bend, Indiana plant in 1963 with production continuing in Ontario, Canada until the company closed in 1966.

The sporty Daytona variant, introduced in 1962, was the Pace Car at the 1962 Indy 500 driven by 1957 Indy 500 winner Sam Hanks.

2021

TRANSATLANTIC TROPHY FOR PRE 1966 TOURING CARS

Callum Lockie and Julian Thomas shared the driving of this second generation Ford Falcon which unfortunately ended in the gravel at Stowe after a coming together with other cars.

The Falcon seems an unlikely rally car, but in the hands of Bo Ljungfeldt, an Alan Mann Racing prepared Falcon (one of eight AMR Falcons in the event) nearly won the 1964 Monte Carlo Rally only being beaten on handicap by the Mini of Paddy Hopkirk.

AMR also prepared and entered a Falcon in the 1967 British Saloon Car Championship driven by Australian Frank Gardner, who won all but one of the 10 rounds to secure the first of his three BSCC championships.

RACE RESULTS Silverstone Classic 2021

Race 1: **Historic Formula Junior**
First: Richard Bradley (Brabham BT2
Second: Cameron Jackson (Brabham BT2)
Third: Alex Ames (Brabham BT6)

Race 2: **MRL Pre-War 'BRDC 500'**
First: Wakeman/Blakeney-Edwards (Frazer Nash TT Replica)
Second: Michael Birch (Talbot AV105 Brooklands)
Third: Clive Morley (Bentley 3/4.5)

Race 3: **Historic Formula 2**
First: Matthew Wrigley (March 782)
Second: Andrew Smith (March 742)
Third: Miles Griffiths (Ralt RT1)

Race 4: **RAC Historic Tourist Trophy (Pre-1963 GT)**
First: Lukas Halusa (Ferrari 250 GT 'Breadvan')
    Second: Cottingham/Stanley (Jaguar E-Type)
        Third: Fisken/Ward (Jaguar E-Type)

Race 5: **Murray Walker Memorial Trophy for Masters Historic Formula One**
First: Michael Lyons (Ensign N180B)
Second: Mike Cantillon (Williams FW07C)
Third: Jamie Constable (Tyrrell 011)

Race 6: **HSCC Thundersports**
First: Tony Sinclair (Lola T292)
Second: Callum Lockie (March 717)
Third: Kevin Cooke (March 75S)

Race 7: **Classic Mini Challenge**
First: Bill Sollis (Morris Mini Cooper S)
Second: Nathan Heathcote (Morris Mini Cooper S)
Third: Chris Middlehurst (Morris Mini Cooper S)

Race 8: **HGPCA Pre-1966 GP Cars**
First: Sam Wilson (Lotus 18 372)
Second: Will Nuthall (Cooper T53)
Third: Rüdiger Friedrichs (Cooper T53)

Race 9: **Transatlantic Trophy for Pre-1966 Touring Cars**
First: Craig Davies (Ford Mustang)
Second: Jewell/Clucas (Ford Lotus Cortina)
Third: Mann/Soper (Ford Mustang)

Race 10: **Masters Endurance Legends**
First: Rob Wheldon (Lola B12/60)
Second: Francois Perrodo (Peugeot 908
Third: Jamie Constable (Pescarolo LMP1)

Race 11: **Yokohama Trophy for Masters Historic Sports Cars**
First: Brundle/Pearson (Lola T70 Mk3B)
Second: Oliver Bryant (Lola T70 Mk3B)
Third: Beighton/Hadfield (Lola T70 Mk3B)

RACE 17: MURRAY WALKER TROPHY FOR MASTERS HISTORIC FORMULA ONE

Start of Sunday's wet race and Lukas Halusa (McLaren M23 (#2), Steve Hartley (McLaren MP4/1 (#77), Jamie Constable (Tyrrell 011 (#99), and Mike Cantillon (Williams FW07/C (#7) lead eventual race winner Michael Lyons in the Ensign N180B (#8).

Race 12: MRL Royal Automobile Club Woodcote & Stirling Moss Trophies

First: Martin O'Connell (Lotus 11)
Second: Roger Wills (Lotus 15)
Third: Ward/Smith (Lister Knobbly)

Race 13: Historic Formula Junior

First: Cameron Jackson (Brabham BT2)
Second: Richard Bradley (Brabham BT2)
Third: Pierre Livingston (Lotus 22)

Race 14: Adrian Flux Trophy for MRL Historic Touring Car Challenge

First: Wright/Coyne (Ford Sierra Cosworth RS500)
Second: Steve Dance (Ford Capri)
Third: Soper/Davies (Ford Sierra Cosworth RS500)

Race 15: Historic Formula 2

First: Andrew Smith (March 742)
Second: Matthew Wrigley (March 742)
Third: Miles Griffiths (Ralt RT1)

Race 16: 60th Anniversary E-Type Challenge

First: Jon Minshaw (Jaguar E-Type)
Second: Ben Mitchell (Jaguar E-Type)
Third: Danny Winstanley (Jaguar E-Typ)e

Race 17: Murray Walker Memorial Trophy for Masters Historic Formula One

First: Michael Lyons (Ensign N180B)
Second: Mike Cantillon (Williams FW07C)
Third: Steve Hartley (McLaren MP4/1)

Race 18: HGPCA Pre-1966 GP Cars

First: Andrew Haddon (Scarab Offenhauser)
Second: Rüdiger Friedrichs (Cooper T53)
Third: Justin Maeers (Cooper T53)

Race 19: International Trophy for Classic GT Cars (pre-1966)

First: Thomas/Lockie (Shelby Daytona Cobra)
Second: Oliver Bryant (AC Cobra)
Third: Alderslade/Jordan (AC Cobra Daytona Coupé)

Race 20: Masters Endurance Legends

First: Francois Perrodo (Peugeot 908)
Second: Shaun Lynn (Peugeot 908)
Third: Jamie Constable (Pescarolo LMP1)

John Davison got it a bit wrong at Club in his TVR Griffith during Friday qualifying for the International Trophy for pre-1966 Classic GT Cars and ended up in the gravel, thankfully without damage to car or driver.

Notwithstanding that little incident he set a time good enough for second on the grid alongside the race-winning Shelby Cobra Daytona of Julian Thomas and Calum Lockie, and brought the TVR home in third place.

CLASSIC SILVERSTONE 2022

August 26th. – August 28th.

Historic Formula Junior races opened proceedings on both Saturday and Sunday with Pole sitter Michael O'Brien taking the win in both races.

Saturday's race saw O'Brien in an epic struggle with first Cameron Jackson who led from the start, only to lose out when lapping back markers and dropped back to finish fourth at the flag. Horatio Fitz-Simon then took the fight to O'Brien, with Sam Wilson joining in, only to retire at Copse on the final lap with suspension breakage, probably caused by bouncing over the kerb at Brooklands. A last corner challenge by Fitz-Simon meant a charge to the line by both drivers resolved in O'Brien's favour by just 0.13 seconds.

Having solved the slight misfire that slowed him down the straights on Saturday, O'Brien roared away from the field in Sunday's Formula junior race with Horatio Fitz-Simon in a lonely second until he pulled off at Brooklands, leaving second placed to be hotly disputed by Sam Wilson, Alex Ames and Tim De Silva who finished in that order, with just 0.4 seconds separating them.

Another double race winner was Ben Mitchell who took the first spot in both HSCC Historic Formula 2 races in his 1977 Martini Mk19/22. Andy Smith (March 782) took the lead in the first race and looked set for the win until he slowed just three laps from the end and pulled into the pits, gifting the race win to Mitchell, from Mathew Watts (March 782) in second and third place finisher David Shaw in yet another March 782

In Sunday's race Mitchell scored a pole to flag victory ahead of Greg Canton who, having taken over David Shaw's drive in the March 78, came from last on the grid to second place. Tim De Silva took the third spot having started second last on the grid.

The Tony Dron Memorial Trophy for MRL Historic Touring Cars had a hectic start in which the second and third cars on the grid (the Ford RS500s of Julian Thomas and David Tomlin (collided at the first corner, eliminating Thomas there and then, although Tomlin continued to take his compulsory pitstop, after which the front left tyre deflated, probably as a result of bodywork damage sustained in the first corner incident.

It looked like it was going to be a Nissan Skyline 1-2-3 finish, until the second place Skyline of Ric Wood coasted to a halt on the Wellington Straight in the last five minutes of the 45 minute race.

Leaving Andy Middlehurst in the original Nissan Skyline which raced in the 1990 Japanese Touring Car Championship (the other two Skylines in the race are recreations) to take the win ahead of the Skyline of Simon Garrard in second ahead of a hard charging Alex Brundle in the Ford Capri RS3100 he shared with Garry Pearson.

Third place Pearson/Brundle Ford Capri RS3100

BRDC 500 for MRL Pre-War Sports Cars. In an entertaining and largely incident-free race featuring some cars nearly a hundred years old, Gregor Fisken and Pat Blakeney-Edwards took Fred Wakeman's 1928 chain-driven Frazer Nash TT Replica to a well-deserved win. Rüdiger Freidrichs secured second spot in the slightly younger Alvis Firefly Special from 1932, while Gareth Burnett in the positively youthful 1939 Alta Sports took the last podium place.

Pat Blakeney -Edwards at the wheel of Fred Wakeman's Frazer Nash

Once again Historic F1 cars featured in two races over the weekend, this time for the Frank Williams Memorial Trophy. Appropriately both races saw a Williams car take the win in the hands of Mike Cantillon driving the ex-Carlos Reuteman Wiliams FW07C from 1982. Streaking away from pole in race 1, Cantillon dominated the race to win by nearly four seconds from Steve Hartley's ex-John Watson McLaren MP4/1 with Ken Tyrrell's Tyrrell 011 seven seconds further back.

Sunday saw the first six finishers from Saturday starting in reverse order on the grid with Mark Hazell's Williams FW07B leading the pack off the start line, but on lap 2 he slipped back behind Jamie Constable (Tyrrell 011) and Steve Brooks (JPS-liveried Lotus 91). By lap 4 Cantillon had taken the lead ahead of the two Tyrrells of Constable and Ken Tyrrell, in which order they stayed until the chequered flag.

Unusually for The Classic we next had a race for a current, or near current, race series — the Masters GT4 Classic Silverstone Challenge. On Saturday a 13 strong grid of cars headed by teenagers Seb Hopkins (in the Team Parker Racing Porsche 718 Cayman GT4 RS CS) and Freddie Tomlinson (in the Team LNT Ginetta G56 GT40). From the start Hopkins took the lead followed by Tomlinson and David Vresky in the Buggyra Racing Mercedes-AMG GT4, and they stayed that way to the flag.

Sunday saw a repeat 1-2; but with Tomlinson taking the win from Hopkins and Aliyyah Koloc taking third spot in the second of the Buggrya Racing's Mercedes AMF GT4s.

The first of the two races for pre-1966 GP cars saw 43 drivers take to the grid in rear and front-engined cars ranging in age from 58 to 69 years old. In the first race Rüdiger Friedrichs (1960 Cooper T53) made a demon start from seventh on the grid to snatch the lead into the first corner, only for pole sitter Will Nuthall (1960 Cooper T53) to out-brake him into Farm and take a lead which was never challenged. Friedrichs was also overtaken by Michael Gans (1964 Cooper T79) on the opening lap and they finished the race in that order.

Sunday's running saw Michael Gans took the lead from Nuthall at Becketts on the first lap only to loose out to Nuthall down the Wellington Straight, with these two finishing in the same order as on Saturday, and Rüdiger Friedrichs also claiming the third position spot again.

MASTERS GT4 CLASSIC SILVERSTONE CHALLENGE

Start of Sunday's GT4 race with the Ginetta of eventual race winner Freddie Tomlinson (#56) alongside the Porsche Cayman of second place man Seb Hopkins (#65). The two Buggyra Racing Mercedes-AMG GT4s of David Vrsecky (#38) and Aliyyah Koloc (#29) on row two finished fourth and third respectively.

HISTORIC FORMULA JUNIOR

Conceived by Count Giovanni "Johnny" Lurani in the late 1950s as an affordable entry-level format for future Italian GP drivers, Formula Junior was quickly recognised by the FIA as a replacement for the outdated Formula 3 category, and became popular throughout Europe.

Following the success of Eric Broadley's Lola Mk.1 sports racer, Broadley diversified into the new Formula Junior category with the Lola Mk.2, a front-engined single seater using a modified Ford 105E engine offset to the right in a complex multi-tube chassis frame with the driver offset to the left.

On June 19th 1960 Peter Ashdown drove a Mk. 2 to the first victory for a single seater Lola at Snetterton, after Ashdown had finished second in the FJ support race for the 1960 Monaco GP, where Stirling Moss took Rob Walker's rear-engined Lotus 18 to a famous victory. The Lotus 18 was also available in a Formula Junior variant, and this and other mid-engined cars soon rendered the front-engined cars uncompetitive in FJ and every other open wheel formula.

The Lola Mk.2 shown here in Swiss racing colours was delivered to its first owner, Helmut Fabian in late 1960 and appears to have had its first race at Monza in 1971. Currently owned by Mahindra de Silva who drove it in both Formula Junior races at Silverstone.

A determined scrap for fourth between the Cooper T53 of Justin Maeers, the Brabham BT3/4 of Tim Child, and the iconic Lotus 25 with which Jim Clark won seven out of the ten F1 Championship races in 1963, driven now by Andy Middlehurst, was resolved in favour of Tim Child just in front of Middlehurst, while Maers was pipped to sixth by Andrew Beaumont in a Lotus 18.

The largest grid of the weekend saw an eclectic mix of 65 cars head out to contest Saturday's International Trophy for pre-1966 Classic GT Cars, with American Ford 4.7 litre V8-engined cars and E-Types dominating the first four rows of the grid, interrupted only by the diminutive 1700cc Ginetta G4R of Mark Halstead and Dan Eagling in fourth.

Pole sitter Julian Thomas in the Shelby Cobra Daytona was beaten away from the lights by second on the grid John Davison driving a TVR Griffith powered by the same V8 as in the Cobra, with another TVR Griffith driven by Mike Whitaker slotting into third. Somewhat predictably the less powerful Ginetta was outgunned by the bigger engined cars and slipped down to 14th spot by the end of lap 1.

Thomas undercut Davison at The Loop on the second lap to take the lead with the Davison and Whitaker TVRs in second and third followed by the first of the Jaguar E-Types driven by James Dodd. Dodd's took the lead after the compulsory pit stops with the Shelby Cobra Daytona, now driven by Callum Lockie back behind Dodd and the two TVRs of Davison and Whitaker. With five minutes to go. Lockie powered the Cobra ahead to take the win from Dodd, Davison and Whitaker.

From pole position on the grid Steve Tandy took the diesel-powered Peugeot 90X from 2011 into a first lap lead in the Masters Endurance Legends race on Saturday, until second place man Tim De Silva in the Pescarolo LMP1 got by under braking for Brooklands on lap 2. At the pit stop Tim's father Harindra took over, but coasted to a stop shortly after taking over the car.

At the flag Tandy was first ahead of Jamie Constable in another Pescarolo LMP1; but a 30 second yellow flag penalty dropped Tandy to second, handing the win to Constable, with Michael Lyons in the Mazda-AER engined Lola B12 third.

Sunday's race saw Jamie Constable take the Pescarolo into the lead from pole, despite a big lock-up at Farm, followed by Steve Tandy's Peugeot and Michael Lyons' Lola, however with 18 minutes left to run a coming together

between Constable and the Steve Osborne (no relation!)/Chris Ward Porsche 911 GT3 at Copse saw the immediate elimination of the Porsche with a broken right rear wheel, and exactly a lap later at the same corner, the Pescarolo came to a stop after the right rear tyre delaminated as a result of that incident.

The resulting long Safety Car period meant just one lap to the finish with an exciting wheel-to-wheel battle between Michael Lyons and Tim De Silva, with De Silva diving past Lyons at the last corner to cross the line ahead, only to be penalised one second for exceeding track limits at that corner and handing the win to Lyons.

Stirling Moss Trophy winner Roger Wills rounds Aintree Corner ahead of the 1952 Cooper Bristol Sports of Chris and Oliver Phillips.

Saturday's racing was brought to an end with the Yokohama Trophy for Masters Sports Car Legends which featured a field largely made up of cars from Chevron and Lola, with the Chevron B19 of Tom Bradshaw on pole.

From the rolling start Bradshaw streaked away opening up a five second gap from Diego Ferrao in the 1973 Lola T292 by lap 2, although by the following lap Alex Brundle had used the 4.7 litre Chevrolet grunt in the Lola T70 to pass Ferrao to take second spot, albeit seven seconds behind the leader.

A Safety Car period from lap 9 to lap 12 bunched the field up; but with a

number of slower cars between Bradshaw and Brundle when they were released, Brundle had his work cut out to catch Bradshaw (a task that became impossible when the big Chevy engine started blowing clouds of smoke under acceleration leading Brundle to pit on the penultimate lap. The drama didn't end though as Bradshaw also started to smoke and slowed on the last lap to cross the line, take the win and almost immediately pull off with collapsed left front suspension.

Another huge grid saw 53 starters for the MRL RAC Woodcote and Stirling Moss Trophies race for 1950s sports cars with James Cottingham leading from pole at the start in the Tojeiro Ecosse Jaguar from the Lister Knobbly of Chris Ward/Rob Smith took the lead at Luffield on the second lap, with New Zealander Roger Wills in a Lotus 15, which was driven by Bruce McLaren in period, in third place.

An Aston off at Copse brought out the Safety Car which lead to an unfortunate incident involving a number of cars in the following crocodile causing the race to be red-flagged. At the restart, with 37 minutes left to run, Roger Wills got the Lotus 15 into second behind Chris Ward in the Lister Knobbly until on lap 7 Ward was passed by both Wills and Cottingham at the end of the Hangar Straight just before his mandatory pit stop when the Willis/Jobstl Lotus 15 took over the lead.

Roger Wills emerged in the lead after the pit stops worked out, and he held the lead to the finish winning the Stirling Moss Trophy, with second place going to Ollie Hancock who took over from John Spiers in the Lister Jaguar Knobbly after a dramatic last few laps battle with Harvey Stanley in the Tojeiro Jaguar he'd shared with James Cottingham.

The Woodcote Trophy section of the race saw a win for the Gregor Fisken/Martin Stretton HWM in a close finish with the Jaguar D-Type driven by John and Gary Pearson.

Jaguar E-Types took the first five places on the grid for the RAC Historic Tourist Trophy race for pre-1963 GT cars with the pole car being the ex-Huffaker Motorsports 1961 E-Type successfully raced in the USA back in the 1960s and here driven by the familiar Cottingham/Stanley pairing.

Ollie Webb in a fixed head coupé E-Type chased after the soft top E-Type of James Cottingham from the start; but the E-Type of Gary Pearson made a very slow start from third on the grid and pulled off track at the first corner.

HSCC HISTORIC FORMULA TWO

Ben Mitchell drove this 1977 Martini MK19/22, owned by Matthew Watts, to victory in both Formula Two Races over the Classic Silverstone weekend.

In 1976 Patrick Tambay raced this car with a V6 Renault engine to third place in the European F2 Championship (Rene Arnoux won the championship in a similar Martini). The following year the Renault engine was replaced with a BMW power unit and driven by Xavier Lapeyre. Watts purchased the car in 2015 and has restored it to its 1977 BMW engined configuration.

Born in Italy 'Tico' Martini grew up on Jersey where he started building karts before founding Automobiles Martini at the Magny-Cours circuit in France. Initially successful in Formula Three, with Jacques Laffite winning the F3 tile in 1973, Martini later moved into Formula Two and then, in 1978 Rene Arnoux made his F1 debut driving the Ford Cosworth DFV engined Martini MK23.

At the flag Harvey Stanley took the win in the Huffaker E-Type from Guy Ziser in the FHC E-Type he'd taken over from Ollie Webb, while a hard fought battle between Richard Cook in a Shelby Cobra and Danny Winstanley in another FHC E-Type went the way of Cook for third place.

Dean Forward was out again in the Thundersports race, this time in the monstrous McLaren M8F, as raced by Peter Revson and Denny Hulme to a 1-2 finish in the 1971 Can-Am Championship, which he had put on pole just over 3 seconds ahead of the Chevron B26 of veteran driver John Burton.

Predictably the McLaren's awesome 8-litre Chevrolet power enabled Forward to run away from Burton and the rest of the field right from the start. Not so predictably, with just four laps completed, the big McLaren slowed dramatically along the Wellington Straight with a broken oil pump drive belt and was passed by Burton and Greg Caton who had taken his March 75S into third from ninth on the grid.

Fire-breathing monster. The McLaren M8F driven by Dean Forward retired from the lead of the Thundersports race after it ate the oil pump drive belt.

After a Safety Car period to remove Paul Cope's March 75S from where it had stopped in the entrance to the National Pits, Greg Caton took the lead until, after a bit of bumping through Brooklands and Luffield, Burton took the lead back between Copse and Maggots. An 'off' at the Loop by Robert Hall in the Shrike P15 brought out the Safety Car where it stayed until the race end, giving victory to John Burton (not bad for an eighty year old!

The weekend's racing came to an end with the Adrian Flux Trophy for Transatlantic pre-1966 Touring Cars. With the first four rows of the grid being an almost solid Ford V8 affair, only broken by the Lotus Cortina of Marcus Jewell and Ben Clucas on the second row, it was no surprise that the leader at the end of the first lap was the Mustang of Steve Soper, followed by James Thorpe (Mustang) and World Touring Car Champion Andy Priaulx in another Mustang.

Soper appeared to have handling problems which allowed Thorpe and then Julian Thomas in the Ford Falcon through. After the pit stops Callum Lockie drove Thomas' Falcon into the lead and took the chequered flag at the end, ahead of Thorpe/Taylor and three other Mustangs.

PJO

RAC HISTORIC TOURIST TROPHY

A puff of tyre smoke from the Jaguar E-Type Huffaker driven by James Cottingham and Harvey Stanley on the way to victory in the Tourist Trophy race. Following is the fifth place AC Cobra of John Spiers and Ollie Hancock.

Fresh of the production line in March 1962 this E-Type was shipped to Kjell Qvale's British Motor Car Distributors in California where it was prepared for the track by Joe Huffaker.

One of the first E-Types on track in North America the car competed in SCCA San Francisco Region events and scored many podium finishes in 1962 and 1963 in the hands of Frank Morrill and Merle Brennan.

DK Engineering purchased the car at an auction in Pebble Beach in 2019, shipped it to the UK and prepared the car for UK historic racing.

Joe Huffaker started building hot rods in California in the late 1940s and by the 1960s Huffaker Engineering had become the largest manufacturer of racing cars in the USA, initially producing cars for Formula Junior and then a series of Sports Racers under the Genie nameplate.

Huffaker Genies used a variety of engines including V8 engines from Ford, Chevrolet, Buick or Oldsmobile and were successfully campaigned in period by many drivers, including Dan Gurney and Pedro Rodriguez.

Keen to promote the Hydrolastic suspension system used on the MG 1100, Qvale commisioned Huffaker to produce three 'MG Liquid Suspension Specials' for the 1964 Indy 500.

Powered by a mid-mounted 1000hp supercharged Offenhauser engine, and with standard Hydrolastic suspension units front and rear, one car driven by Walt Hangsen was running fourth in the race; but a lengthy pit stop dropped the car to 13th at the finish. A second car driven by Bob Vieth finished in 19th spot; but the third car was crashed in qualifying by Pedro Rodriguez.

RAC HISTORIC TOURIST TROPHY

Kevin Kivlochan's Morgan Plus 4 Supersports "*Choc Ices*" (#99), leads the Lotus Elite of Paul Garside (#14), Richard Cook's Shelby Cobra (#72), and the E-Type of Gregor Fisken (#61) into Luffield.

Originally a 1954 model this car was converted to its current fixed roof race specification in 1961 by Lawrence Tune for the then owner Peter Marten who competed in many races that year in the UK and Europe, including the Grand Prix de Spa (where it acquired its *Choc Ices* nickname, supposedly from an unrepeatable joke told by a mechanic) and the Nürburgring 1000 kilometres.

Kivlochan acquired the car in 2022 and returned the paintwork to its original Avian Blue colour from the British Racing Green to which a previous owner had changed it.

RAC HISTORIC TOURIST TROPHY

Richard Cook hard at work behind the wheel of the Shelby Cobra on his way to a third place finish.

AC Cars had been using the Bristol straight six engine in their Ace roadster, but with the discontinuation of that engine in 1961 they switched to the 2.5 litre Ford Zephyr engine. American racer Carroll Shelby saw the potential for a big V8 in the lightweight Ace chassis and asked AC to build an Ace modified to accept such an engine. The modified car was shipped to Shelby's works in Los Angeles where a Ford Windsor 3.6 litre V8 was installed, thus was born the first Shelby Cobra Later models used larger Ford V8s up to the 7.0 litre (427 cu in.). Cook's Cobra has a 4.3 litre engine.

MASTERS ENDURANCE LEGENDS

The number 5 may give a clue that this car was driven by Nigel Mansell; but there are actually three Mansells written on the side, because this Ginetta Zytek was entered for the European Le Mans Series in 2010 by Beechdean Mansell Motorsport to be driven by Nigel and his sons Leo and Greg.

Greg took a sixth and seventh place finish at Paul Ricard and the Hungaroring before all three Mansells were slatted to drive for the Le Mans 24 hours.

The team qualified 18th on the grid; but after only 17 minutes of racing, with Nigel at the wheel, a puncture led to high speed impacts with barriers on both sides of the track, leaving Mansell concussed and later suffering from amnesia. As part of his recovery programme Mansell practised magic tricks at which he became skilled enough to join the Magic Circle.

Developed to meet the new LMP1 regulations for 2009, the Ginett Zytek GZ09S used a 4.5 litre Zyteck ZJ458 V8 developing 635 bhp, and made its race debut with Straka Racing at the opening round of the 2009 Le Mans Series season, the 100Km of Catalunya, driven by Nick Leventis, Peter Hardman, and Danny Watts. After Watts put the new car on pole, the team eventually finished fifth.

MASTERS ENDURANCE LEGENDS

Mike Newton drove his ex-RML MG-Lola EX257 to seventh in Saturday's race and 11th on the Sunday, 18 years after driving the same car at Le Mans.

MG returned to Le Mans in 2001 with two MG-Lola EX257 entered by MG Sport and Racing, the factory team. Although Mark Blundell put one of the cars on pole for the LMP675 Class, and recorded the fastest lap in that class, both cars retired, a feat repeated in 2002 when Anthony Reid took the class pole and fastest lap; but again both cars retired.

MG management decided that two failed attempts at Le Mans were enough and withdrew from competition, although customer teams such as RML (Ray Mallock Limited) in Europe, and Dyson Racing in the USA continued to campaign the EX257 with some success.

RML entered this EX257 at Le Mans in 2004, driven by Newton, with Thomas Erdos and Nathan Kinch. After 256 laps engine problem forced retirement. RML returned to Le Mans in 2005 with an MG EX264, effectively a modified Lola B05/40. Newton and Erdos were joined by Warren Hughes and were rewarded with 20th place, and the LMP2 Class win, at the finish.

MASTERS ENDURANCE LEGENDS

In this Ferrari 458 GT3 Andie Stokoe and David McDonald won the G2/GT3 Class in both of the weekend's races.

Introduced in 2011 the GT3 racing version of the 458 Italia was immediately successful on track with a car entered by SOFREV Auto Sport Promotion and driven by Franck Morel, Guillaume Moreau, Ludovic Badey, and Jean-Luc Beaubelique winning the Pro-Am class of the 2011 Spa 24 Hours, a round of the Blancpain Endurance series.

Ferrari 458 GT3s won the same Pro-Am class at Spa for the next four years.

MASTERS ENDURANCE LEGENDS

Wayne Marrs at the wheel of this Dodge Viper GTS-R seen during Friday qualifying put the car in a mid-field position on the grid; but in Saturday's race expired with just a few laps left to run and did not appear for Sunday's race.

The first public appearance of the Dodge Viper with its thundering 8 litre V10 was at the Indianapolis Motor Speedway in 1991 when Carroll Shelby drove a pre-production model as the Pace Car for that year's Indy 500.

It was not until 1996 that a racing version (the Viper GTS-R) was unveiled. Developed jointly by Chrysler, Oreca and Reynard Motorsport, the GTS-R's first race was the 24 Hours of Daytona where a car entered by Canaska Southwind finished in 29th spot. Canaska Southwind and Oreca entered two cars each for the 1996 Le Mans 24 Hours, three of which finished, with the Canaska Southwind car driven by Price Cobb, Mark Dismore and Shawn Hendricks finishing in tenth place.

MASTERS ENDURANCE LEGENDS

The ex-Felbermayr-Proton Porsche 997 GT3-RSR driven by Steve Osborne (no relation to the author) and Rob Smith won the G1/GT2 class on Saturday but was eliminated in an unfortunate collision at Copse with race leader Jamie Constable's Pescarolo LMP1 during Sunday's race, which also eliminated the Pescarolo exactly one lap later.

Team Felbermayr-Proton ran Porsche 911s in the European Le Mans series, including the 2010 Le Mans 24 Hours, where car #88, driven by Austrian industrialist Horst Felbermayr, his son Horst Jnr., and Slovakian Miro Konopka, finished 24th overall and 8th in class.

MASTERS ENDURANCE LEGENDS

Michael Lyons in this Mazda (AER) engined Lola B12/80 took the win in Sunday's race after Tim De Silva, who crossed the finish line first, was penalised one second for exceeding track limits at the final corner.

Mazda Motorsports entered two cars for the 2016 IMSA WeatherTech SportsCar Championship in the USA. Car #55 driven by Jonathan Bomarito and Tristan Nunez and #70 with Joel Miller and Tom Long sharing the driving.

HGPCA PRE-1966 GRAND PRIX CARS

What's an Indy 500 car doing in the race for pre-1966 GP cars? Between 1950 and 1955 the Indianapolis 500 race was part of the F1 World Championship and so any car that ran at Indianapolis during those years is eligible.

In 1954 the Indy 500 was the second round of that year's F1 season and this Offenhauser-engined Kurtis-Kraft KK500C was driven to sixth place by Fred Agabashian. Walt Faulkner finished fifth in the same car the following year.

Overall this car raced at Indianapolis five times between 1954 and 1959, and also competed in the second of the unique *Race of Two Worlds* events at Monza in 1958 where it was driven by Jimmy Reece.

HGPCA PRE-1966 GRAND PRIX CARS

Nick Fennell drove the Lotus 25 to second in the first of the races for pre-1966 GP Cars, for both front and rear-engined cars, and fourth in the third race for rear-engined cars only.

If John Cooper revolutionised F1 by placing the engine behind the driver in 1957, then Colin Chapman started the second revolution in 1962 with the monocoque structure of the Lotus 25 which made the car stronger, lighter and more aerodynamic than the tubular spaceframe chassis used in the preceding Lotus 24, and all other then current GP cars.

A sensation on its debut at the opening race of the 1962 season in Holland (not least to those privateer teams who had just bought Lotus 24s!), the 25 proved fast with Jim Clark claiming third on the grid and sprinting away into the lead from the start until clutch problems dropped him back down the field to eventually finish ninth. Clark took pole in six of that season's nine races, winning three of them; but failed to finish in another three which gifted the driver's crown to Graham Hill.

In 1963 the 25's reliability was improved and Clark drove the Lotus 25 to victory in seven of the season's ten races to win that year's driver's championship from Graham Hill in second place, with Lotus also winning the Constructor's Championship. Clark was set to retain his World Champion title in 1964 when an engine failure at the last round in Mexico dropped him to third in the championship after John Surtees and Graham Hill.

1965 saw Clark takes his second World Championship driving both the Lotus 25 and the newer Lotus 33, with the 25's last F1 win at the French GP in June 1965.

Jaguar XK140 Gomm Special driven by Rick and Joe Willmott. Gomm Metal Developments constructed this bodywork in 1955 and it was originally fitted to an Alta single seater GP chassis which the owner wanted to use as a road car.

The bodywork was re-discovered in the 1980s and Charles Fripp, from Hampshire based Jaguar XK specialists Twyford Moors, realised that it would fit a Jaguar XK140 chassis as the wheelbase was almost the same. The resulting car was campaigned by Fripp until purchased by the current owner Rick Willmott in 2018.

If there is a common thread running through UK motorsport from the 1950s to the 1990s it is probably Maurice "Mo" Gomm's company Gomm Metal Developments (GMD), which fabricated chassis, bodyshells and components for many of the leading teams of the day, helping many fledgling constructors on the way.

When Eric Broadley built his first Lola he turned to Gomm to make the body panels. Ken Tyrrell came calling to get GMD to fabricate the monocoque for Tyrrell's first eponymous F1 car, the Tyrrell 001. Ford Escort rally car shells were built by GMD, who were also heavily involved in the Le Mans GT40 programme.

During these five decades Gomm Metal Developments were associated with motorsport in many disciplines from F1 through to Can Am, including Indy 500 wining cars, successful World Cup Rally teams, and even built the five *Chitty Chitty Bang Bang* chassis and bodies to which Alan Mann fitted the various fripperies required for filming.

2022

MRL RAC WOODCOTE TROPHY & STIRLING MOSS TROPHY

The James Thorpe/Sean McInerney 1955 Lister Jaguar 'Flat Iron', sporting light collision damage, heads into The Loop ahead of Rick and Joe Willmott's Jaguar XK140 Gomm Special. Mo Gomm is the connection between these two cars as the unique aluminium bodywork of the Lister, which gave it the nickname 'Flat Iron', was also constructed by GMD.

HCH 736 was originally powered by a Bristol engine and driven by drivers including Roy Salvadori until crashed heavily at the 1956 British GP meeting by Austen Nurse. Rebuilt with a Jaguar XK engine and the new Thom Lucas designed bodywork, the car was campaigned under the Equipe Devone banner by Archie Scott-Brown who took 11 wins out of 14 races in 1957.

Bruce Halford and Brian Naylor drove at Le Mans in 1958 to a 13th place finish (the only Lister-Jaguar to have finished at Le Mans.

It was later sold to the Border Reivers team whose new driver Jim Clark, when picking the car up, drove it on the road back from Luton to Berwick, and reputedly overtook a hard-driven Ford Thunderbird on the A1 at 150 mph — different times! Clark scored multiple victories in HCH 736 and he is said to have credited the car with teaching him the most about driving a racing car.

MRL RAC WOODCOTE TROPHY & STIRLING MOSS TROPHY

1952 Frazer Nash Le Mans Replica MkII driven by Cliff Gray ahead of the Keers-Trafford/Emmerling Elva MkV.

In 1949, at the first post-war running of the Le Mans 24 Hours, a Frazer Nash High Speed driven by Frazer Nash MD Harold Aldington and Norman Culban came home in third spot. Frazer Nash named subsequent cars as Le Mans Replicas to commemorate that result.

XMG 6 was driven by Stirling Moss at the 1952 Prix de Monte Carlo, a support race for the GP, where he placed the car on pole but retired from the race when battling for second. Tony Brooks in another Le Mans replica won that race.

MRL RAC WOODCOTE TROPHY & STIRLING MOSS TROPHY

Paul Griffin in the 1954 Connaught AL/SR (#31) leads the Nick Wigley/Barry Cannell 1952 Frazer Nash Le Mans Mk2. They finished the race in the same order.

The Connaught AL/SR is a two seat sports racer developed from Connaught's single seater F2 cars which were popular with privateers for the 1952 Formula One series that was actually run to F2 regulations. The cars were competitive but outclassed by the new four cylinder Ferrari 500 which won all eight races of the season.

Connaught's best F1 performance was in 1955 at the non-championship Syracuse Grand Prix where dental student Tony Brooks, in his first GP drive, put a Connaught third on the grid and scored a resounding win over the Maserati of Luigi Musso. The first GP win for a British driver in a British car since Henry Segrave won the 1924 San Sebastien GP in a Sunbeam.

In 1954 two of the team's AL single seaters were converted to two-seat sports racers and renamed as AL/SR, with their best result being a sixth place, and class win, at the 1955 Goodwood 9 hour race driven by Les Leston and Archie Scott-Brown. The two cars were also entered for the infamous 1955 Le Mans 24 Hours but neither car finished.

HISTORIC FORMULA JUNIOR

Front-engined Elva FJ100 (#22) of Nigel Lackford about to be swallowed up by the rear-engined Brabham BT6 (#88) of Alex Ames who finished eleventh in Saturday's race and third on Sunday.

Frank Nicholls founded Elva in 1955, naming his company after the French phrase *Elle va* (She goes). Elva initially produced sports racing cars which achieved success in the hands of Archie Scott-Brown, Stuart Lewis-Evans and others. In 1959 the company's only single seater racer, the FJ100, was introduced. Conforming to the then current Formula Junior regulations, the front-engined FJ100 was powered by a BMC A Series engine, with later models using a two-stroke DKW engine.

Introduced just as the rear-engine revolution, pioneered by Cooper and Lotus, took place meant that the FJ100 enjoyed limited success.

HISTORIC FORMULA JUNIOR

Nic Carlton-Smith at the wheel of this Kieft FJ scored a mid-field finish in race one, but DNF'd in the second race.

Steel industrialist Cyril Kieft founded Kieft Cars in 1950 and achieved considerable success in the Formula 3 class with drivers including Stirling Moss. Moss and his manager Ken Gregory were so impressed with the cars that they became directors of the company.

By the end of the decade Kieft's fortunes had faded and the company was bought in 1960 by John Turney and Lionel Mayman (gentleman racer and husband of Pauline Mayman who was Pat Moss' navigator in 1962). Mayman himself drove this car in 1961.

TONY DRON MEMORIAL TROPHY FOR MRL HISTORIC TOURING CARS

The Banks' Brothers Alfaholics Alfa Romeo Giulia Sprint GTA gets the front wheel airborne at Brooklands corner.

The GTA, A for Alleggerita (Lightweight in Italian), was developed from the Giulia Sprint for motorsport by Autodelta, Alfa Romeo's racing division, and featured aluminium, rather than steel, outer body panels; a twin plug per cylinder head; larger Weber carburettors and closer ratio gears.

The GTA was immediately highly successful in competition winning the 1966 European Touring Car Challenge in the hands of Andrea de Adamich.

TONY DRON MEMORIAL TROPHY FOR MRL HISTORIC TOURING CARS

Two contrasting racing Capris. The Hermetite-liveried car (#14) driven by John Spiers and Ollie Hancock followed by the Broadspeed Capri (#88) of Richard Kent and Chris Ward during Friday qualifying. Both cars did not finish in Saturday's race. The Sheraton's BMW E30 lurking in the background finished the race in 25th place.

Hermetite sponsorship was seen on the Capri driven by Holman Blackburn in the 1974 British Saloon Car Championship which changed from Group 2 to mildly uprated Group 1 specifications in order to reduce costs, the result was a highly competitive championship involving many manufacturers. Bernard Unett took the drivers title in a Hillman Avenger, with Andy Rouse (Triumph Dolomite Sprint) in second and Stuart Graham (Chevrolet Camaro Z28) taking the third spot.

TONY DRON MEMORIAL TROPHY FOR MRL HISTORIC TOURING CARS

David Tomlin qualified this Ford RS500 on the second row of the grid but tangled with the Kaliber RS500 of Julian Thomas at the first corner, which relegated him to last place. Fought back up the field; but eventually retired with a puncture resulting from bodywork damage in that first corner collision.

Batibouw livery featured on the Andy Rouse Engineering entered RS500 driven by Alain Semoulin, Jesus Pareja, and Thierry Tassin to sixth place in the 1987 Spa 24 Hour race.

TONY DRON MEMORIAL TROPHY FOR MRL HISTORIC TOURING CARS

Second place finisher, the Nissan Skyline R32 GT-R (#37) of Simon Garrad passes the Opel Commodore B GSE (#30) driven by Peter Fisk which finished towards the rear of the field but fourth in class.

The Nissan Skyline R32 (referred to as Godzilla, because it's a fire-breathing monster from Japan) dominated the Japanese Touring Car Championship, winning in every year from 1989 to 1993. Success in other countries included winning the Bathurst 1000 in 1991 and 1992, the Spa 24 Hours in 1991, the 1991 Australian Touring Car Championship, driven by New Zealander Jim Richards, and numerous wins in UK and Europe for three cars prepared and entered by Janspeed.

The inaugural Willhire 24 Hour relay race at Snetterton in 1980 was won by the two-car team of Opel Commodores driven by (among others) Pete Hall and Phil Dowsett. The same Commodores also secured the win at the same event the following year.

HSCC THUNDERSPORTS

John Burton at the wheel of his Chevron B26 was the class of the field in the Thundersports race, after Dean Forward's McLaren retired, to take a well deserved and popular win. 80 year old Burton started racing in the 1960s and has competitively raced this Chevron for many years.

Chevron introduced the B26 in 1973 with an aluminium monocoque rather than the spaceframe chassis of the previous B23 model. Its race debut was at the Kayalami 9 Hours in 1973 (in Team Gunston colours). Driven by John Watson and Ian Schekter, the pair were looking good for a first-time-out win for the B26 until the engine overheated which dropped them to fifth at the chequered flag.

2022

Rhodesian racing driver John Love is probably best known in the UK as the winner of the 1962 British Saloon Car Championship (the first non-Brit to do so) driving a Mini Cooper; but he also competed in Formula One races between 1962 and 1972.

At the 1968 South African GP Love entered two cars (a Brabham and an LDS), driven by himself and Sam Tingle, under the name of Team Gunston painted in the colours of Gunston, a South African cigarette brand, thus becoming the first F1 team to sport a sponsor's livery.

Team Gunston's orange and chocolate colours also appeared on F500, F2 and sports racing cars in South Africa as seen on the Lola T212 of Greg Furst and the Chevron B19 (#12) with Jamie Thwaites at the wheel seen here on the run down to Vale from Stowe, followed by the Osella PA3 (#14) driven by John Spiers, Kevin Cooke in a March 75S, and the De Silva's Taydec Mk.3 (#2).

FRANK WILLIAMS MEMORIAL TROPHY FOR MASTER RACING LEGENDS

Steve Brooks piloted the1982 Lotus 91 to take fourth place in both of the weekend's Historic Formula One races.

1982 was the last F1 season before 'ground effect' cars were banned and the Lotus 91 with its very long side pods produced a lot of downforce; but was challenging to drive with ultra-stiff suspension and somewhat unpredictable aerodynamics.

However, team drivers Nigel Mansell and Elio de Angelis scored enough points between them for Lotus to take fifth place in the Constructors championship. At the Austrian Grand Prix de Angelis took a notable first place, the last Lotus win before Lotus founder Colin Chapman suffered a fatal heart attack in December 1982.

2022

FRANK WILLIAMS MEMORIAL TROPHY FOR MASTER RACING LEGENDS

Alejandro Chahwan at the wheel of a 1981 March 811.

Practically a copy of the Williams FW07, the 811 was designed by Robin Herd, Gordon Coppuck, and Adrian Reynard and manufactured for John Macdonald's RAM Racing, although as 'customer' cars had been banned in FI the team entered as March Grand Prix, legally and organisationally independent of March Engineering.

Driven in period by Derek Daly and Eliseo Salazar the cars were notoriously uncompetitive and unreliable, with only Salazar qualifying in one out of the first six championship races, at the San Marino GP where he retired 38 laps in.

After the Monaco GP Salazar left, taking his sponsorship money to Ensign, leaving Daly as the sole driver for the rest of the season. At the British GP, in the Reynard revised chassis, Daly had his best result of the season finishing in seventh spot, just out of the points, meaning that RAM Racing (March Grand Prix) scored no points in that year's Constructors championship.

HSCC HISTORIC FORMULA 2

Jeremy Caine scored a class win in the second of the weekend's Historic F2 races in this March 712 wearing the 1971 livery of the Motul/Politoys sponsored Frank Williams Racing Team.

The March 712 was the most popular F2 car in the 1971 European F2 season used not just by the works team but also many others, including the Frank Williams Racing Team cars driven by Henri Pescarolo and Derek Bell.

"SuperSwede" Ronnie Peterson secured the 1971 F2 Driver's Title win in a works March 712, with Derek Bell posting the best result for a Williams March 712 driver of 13th in the Championship.

2022

Henri Pescarolo in a Frank Williams Racing Team March 712 during the Jochen Rindt Memorial Trophy F2 race run over two heats and a final at Thruxton, Easter Monday 1971. Pescarolo won heat two, but only completed four laps in the final before the engine blew. The Trophy was claimed by Graham Hill who was first in both heat one and the final in a Rondel Racing Brabham BT36.

HSCC HISTORIC FORMULA 2

David Tomlin's Motul Rondel M1 in the Motul/Radio Luxembourg '208' livery at speed during Sunday's running of the Historic F2 race in which he finished in ninth place.

Henri Pescarolo unites the two photos on this spread as he drove a March 712 and a Motul Rondel M1 in the European F2 Championships between 1971 and 1973.

After running Brabham B36s in F2 in 1971 and 1972, Rondel Racing built their own car for the 1973 season designed by ex-Brabham aerodynamicist Ray Jessop. Pescarolo and Bob Wolleck scored a 1-2 finish for Rondel with the M1 at Thruxton in April 1973, with Wolleck taking sixth spot in the European F2 Championship.

IGNITION GP 1990s FORMULA ONE - DEMONSTRATION

The result of a collaboration between Supercar Driver (www.supercar-driver.com) and ex F1 test driver Jonathan Kennard, Ignition GP brings together Grand Prix cars from one of the most exciting F1 periods (1989-1997) in a series of demonstration events. With turbocharged engines banned, 3.5 litre naturally-aspirated engines with between 8 and 12 cylinders ushered in a new, noisier era for F1.

BRABHAM BT 60B, 1992

The BT60B was the last Brabham Formula One car built by Motor Racing Developments Ltd., the company founded by Jack Brabham and Ron Tauranac in 1960 to design and build racing cars under the Brabham name.

Designed by Tim Densham and powered by a 3.5 litre Judd V10, the BT60B added nothing to the previously illustrious Brabham career in 1992. After finishing in last place at the season opening South African GP in the hands of Eric van de Poele, the team did not qualify for further races until the British GP when F1 rookie Damon Hill qualified 26th and finished in 16th place.

Hill also scored the team's best 1992 result at the Hungarian GP taking the car to 11th spot. This was also the Brabham team's last appearance in F1 and the company went into administration later that year (a sad end to a 30-year F1 history during which they scored four F1 Drivers Championship titles and two Constructors titles). To date Jack Brabham is the only driver to have won the world title in a car bearing his own name.

2022

2022

MINARDI M198, 1998

Giancarlo Minardi founded his eponymously named team in 1980 and had four successful seasons in Formula Two, with their best result being a win for Michelle Alboreto at Misano in 1981 driving a BMW-engined Minardi FLY281.

Moving up to F1 in 1985 Minardis had little success, although Pierluigi Martini did manage to lead a lap of the 1989 Portuguese GP, and also put a Minardi on the front row of the grid for the 1990 United States GP in Phoenix, eventually finishing in seventh.

The Minardi Team continued in F1 to 2005, latterly under the ownership of Paul Stoddart, until Red Bull purchased the team and renamed it Scuderia Torro Rosso.

Race 1: **Historic Formula Junior**
First: Michael O'Brien (Brabham BT6)
Second: Horatio Fitz-Simon (Lotus 22)
Third: Tim De Silva (Brabham BT2)

Race 2: **HSCC Historic Formula 2**
First: Ben Mitchell (Martini MK 19/22)
Second: Matthew Watts (March 782s)
Third: David Shaw (March 782)

Race 3: **Tony Dron Memorial Trophy for MRL Historic Touring Cars**
First: Andy Middlehurst (Nissan Skyline)
Second: Simon Garrad (Nissan Skyline R32)
Third: Pearson/Brundle (Ford Capri RS3100)

Race 4: **MRL Pre-War Sports Cars 'BRDC 500'**
First: Fisken/Blakeney-Edwards (Frazer Nash TT Replica - Supersport')
Second: Rüdiger Friedrichs (Alvis Firefly Special)
Third: Gareth Burnett (Alta Sports)

Race 5: **Frank Williams Memorial Trophy for Masters Racing Legends F1**
First: Mike Cantillon (Williams FW07C)
Second: Steve Hartley (McLaren MP4/1)
Third: Ken Tyrrell (Tyrrell 011)

Race 6: **Masters GT4 Classic Silverstone Challenge**
First: Seb Hopkins (Porsche 718 Cayman GT4 RS CS)
Second: Freddie Tomlinson (Ginetta G56 GT4)
Third: David Vrsecky (Mercedes-AMG GT4)

Race 7: **HGPCA Pre 1966 Grand Prix Cars**
First: Will Nuthall (Cooper T53)
Second: Michael Gans (Cooper T79)
Third: Rüdiger Friedrichs (Cooper T53)

Race 8: **International Trophy for Classic GT Cars (Pre 1966)**
First: Thomas/Lockie (Shelby American Cobra Daytona)
Second: James Dodd (Jaguar E-Type)
Third: John Davison (TVR Griffith)

Race 9: **Masters Endurance Legends**
First: Jamie Constable (Pescarolo LMP1)
Second: Steve Tandy (Peugeot 90X)
Third: Michael Lyons (Lola B12/80)

Race 10: **Yokohama Trophy for Masters Sports Car Legends**
First: Tom Bradshaw(Chevron B19)
Second: Claridge/Gomes (Chevron B23)
Third: Beighton/Hadfield (Lola T70 Mk3B)

Race 11: **Historic Formula Junior**
First: Michael O'Brien (Brabham BT6)
Second: Sam Wilson (Cooper T59)
Third: Alex Ames (Brabham BT6)

Race 12: **MRL Royal Automobile Club Woodcote & Stirling Moss Trophies**
First: Roger Wills (Lotus 15)
Second: Spiers/Hancock (Lister Knobbly)
Third: Cottingham/Stanley (Tojeiro Ecosse Jaguar)

Race 13: HSCC Historic Formula 2
First: Ben Mitchell (Martini MK 19/22)
Second: Greg Caton (March 783)
Third: Tim De Silva (Chevron B35)

Race 14: Royal Automobile Club Historic Tourist Trophy (MRL Pre '63 GT)
First: Cottingham/Stanley (Jaguar E-Type Huffake)
Second: Webb/Ziser (Jaguar E-Type FHCi)
Third: Richard Cook (Shelby AC Cobra)

Race 15: Frank Williams Memorial Trophy for Masters Racing Legends F1
First: Mike Cantillon (Williams FW07C)
Second: Steve Hartley (McLaren MP4/1)
Third: Ken Tyrrell (Tyrrell 011)

Race 16: HGPCA Pre 1966 Grand Prix Cars
First: Will Nuthall (Cooper T53)
Second: Michael Gans (Cooper T79)
Third: Rüdiger Friedrichs (Cooper T53)

Race 17: Masters Endurance Legends
First: Michael Lyons (Lola B12/80)
Second: Timothy De Silva (Pescarolo LMP1)
Third: Steve Tandy (Peugeot 90X)

Race 18: HSCC Thundersports
First: John Burton (Chevron B26)
Second: Gregory Caton (March 75S)
Third: Claridge/Gomes (Chevron B23)

Race 19: Masters GT4 Classic Silverstone Challenge
First: Freddie Tomlinson (Ginetta G56 GT4)
Second: Seb Hopkins (Porsche 718 Cayman GT4 RS CS)
Third: Iiyyah Koloc (Mercedes-AMG GT4)

Race 20: Adrian Flux Trophy for Transatlantic Pre '66 Touring Cars
First: Thomas/Lockie (Ford Falcon)
Second: Thorpe/Quaife(Ford Mustang)
Third: McInerney/Keen (Ford Mustang)

HISTORIC FORMULA JUNIOR (QUALIFYING)

Stuart Tizard's Cooper T56 (#33) and Alex Ames in a Brabham BT6 (#88) flash past the scrutineering bay in the National Paddock at Copse corner.

Saturday's running of the Masters Racing Legends F1 race. Pole sitter Ken Tyrrell in the Tyrrell 011 (#23) leads Steve Hartley's McLaren MP4/1 (#77) into Copse corner on the opening lap, followed by Martin Stretton in the Benetton liveried Tyrrell 012, Mike Cantillon's Williams FW07C, and Jamie Constable's Tyrrell 011 (#99). Cantillon would finish first on the road but was later disqualified for a technical infringement, handing the win to Ken Tyrrell.

Once again Classic motor racing returned to a bustling Silverstone circuit over the August Bank Holiday weekend for a true festival of racing, rocking, and family entertainment (fittingly now re-branded as the Silverstone Festival.

With races from Formula Junior to Formula One, and practically everything inbetween, race fans were entertained all weekend, with a few rain showers thrown in to spice up the on-track action. As in previous years Formula Junior started the day's racing on both Saturday and Sunday, with Sam Wilson (Lotus 20/22) taking the win in both races, followed by Alex Ames (Brabham BT6) and Sam Harrison (Renmax BN1-2) in Saturday's race. Ames was relegated to third in Sunday's running with Horatio Fitz-Simon (Lotus 22) taking the second spot.

Next up on Saturday was the HSCC Thundersports race where pole sitter Mike Lyons in the Ibec 308LM was beaten off the line at the start by Mark Williams in the massive 8 litre March 717 Can-Am car although, after Lyons was eased on to the grass entering Vale on the first lap, he soon took the lead. A few laps later Williams spun the March at Becketts letting Dan Eagling's Royale RP17 through into second place. With just three minutes left to run Williams drove the March into retirement in the National Pits elevating the Lola T70B of Ross Hyett into third place at the finish. Second place man Eagling was the only runner not lapped by Mike Lyons.

Star drive of the weekend followed in the Derek Bell Trophy race for HSCC Formula Libre. Henry Chart was entered to drive his newly-purchased Modus M1; but the engine blew (rod through block) during qualifying. Overnight Simon Hadfield's team resurrected their Trojan T101 Formula 5000 car (which had not turned a wheel for some years, and Chart started that car from the back of the grid, (having sat in the car for the first time 30 minutes before the race) charging through the field to fifth place at the end of the first lap, second place on lap 2, and taking the lead from lap 6 to the flag! The following day he underscored his supremacy with a pole to flag victory in the second Formula Libre race.

After the rain, and Mark Goodyear's car stuck in the gravel at Luffield, brought a red flag end to the Formula Libre race the Touring Car Challenge cars came out on to a very wet track between Brooklands and Becketts, although dry elsewhere. After a couple of sighting laps behind the safety car the two front row cars, the Sierra RS500s of Paul Mensley and Julian Thomas pulled away from the field until the Kent/Osborne Capri parked at the end of the Hamilton Straight brought out the safety car. Andy Middlehurst in the Nissan Skyline took over the lead, but missed the pit stop window, incurring a penalty which became irrelevant when the Skyline broke towards the end of the race handing the victory to a jubilant Wim Kuijl in a Ford Capri.

Saturday's Formula One race saw pole sitter Ken Tyrrell lead a stellar grid of Cosworth DFV engined F1 cars from 1966 to 1983. A long safety car period to recover Werner

D'Ansembourg's Williams FW07C from its stationary position on the outside of The Loop bunched up the field, and at the restart Mike Cantillon shot up from fourth to take the lead by Brooklands. A stationary car next to the International pits brought out a second safety car under which the race finished with Cantillon ahead of Tyrrell. However, Cantillon was later disqualified for having the rear wing too high, handing the official win to Tyrrell.

A partly wet track for the second F1 race saw the whole field on wets apart from Michael Lyons (JPS Lotus 92). A gamble that paid off as he lead from start to finish, except for one lap when Jamie Constable got ahead only to spin the lead away round The Loop;

The Masters GT Trophy saw a Lambo-dominated grid with the first four rows filled with Lamborghini Huracans, apart from a solitary Aston Martin in fifth spot. Craig Wilkins (Lamborghini Huracan Super Trofeo Evo) quickly established a lead from the start which he never relinquished, apart from the mandatory pit stop, until the finish, An epic struggle through the second half of the race between the Lamborghini Huracans of Jason

MASTERS GT TROPHY
Race winner Craig Wilkins at the wheel of this Lamborghini Huracan Super Trofeo Evo

McInulty and Alistair Mackinnon was resolved when Mackinnon shouldered his way past on the outside at The Loop on the final lap.

The HGPCA pre-1966 GP cars race was led for many laps by pole sitter Will Nuthall in a Cooper T53 from Charlie Martin in another Cooper T53 until the seventh lap when Nuthall pulled into the its to retire. Martin then had an unchallenged run to the flag, with the second placed car, the Lotus 25 of Nick Fennel one lap adrift.

On Sunday the HGPCA ran two more races, one for front-engined cars from 1948-1960, and the second for rear engined GP cars. In the front-engine race John Spiers led from pole in the Maserati 250F only to spin at Becketts letting Rod Jolley in the shiny silver Lister Jaguar Monza GP through to the lead, followed by Klaus Lehr in another Maserati 250F. Having recovered from his spin Spiers regained the lead with 3 minutes left with

Mark Shaw in the Scarab Offenhauser closely following with Shaw finding a way past Spiers at Farm on the final lap.

The third HGPCA race, for rear engined GP cars, saw almost a re-run of Saturday's race with Charlie Martin winning again after a many laps tussle with Tim Child in a Brabham BT3/4, beating Child to the line by 1.4 seconds.

International Trophy for pre-1966 Classic GT Cars. John Davidson in a TVR Griffith beat pole sitter Julian Thomas' Shelby Cobra Daytona away from the start, although Thomas got back in front along the National Pits straight first time round. Nigel Greensall in another TVR Griffith later challenged for the lead taking over the number one spot until the mandatory pit stops, after which the Daytona, now driven by Callum Lockie, regained the lead which it held until the chequered flag.

The spirit of Le Mans returned to Silverstone in the 100th anniversary year of that 24 Hour race with the two Endurance Legends races. In the first race on Saturday Harindra de Silva in a Pescarolo LMP1 led away from pole; but was swiftly overtaken by Steve Brooks' diesel powered Peugeot 90X, until the lead was taken by Jonathan Kennard in the Acura LMP2 ARX01b. The Acura however broke on its tenth lap handing the lead back to Steve Brooks who was chased to the flag by a spirited drive from Tim de Silva, who had taken over the Pescarolo from his father at the mandatory pit stop.

Sunday's race started under the safety Car as the Claude Bovet/David McDonald Aston Martin GT3 had ground to a standstill on the warm up lap at Village corner with a loose front wheel. When racing proper started the Lola Aston Martin driven by Christophe d'Ansembourg collided with the second placed Pescarolo of Harindra de Silva at The Loop spinning the Pescarolo back down the field. The two Peugeots of Steve Brooks and Stuart Wiltshire held first and second, apart from the pitstops, to the finish. Another spirited drive from Tim de Silva saw him get the Pescarolo up to 14th place before the car expired with just a handful of laps to go.

Last race on Saturday was the Yokohama Trophy for Sports Car Legends. David Hart took his Ferrari 512M from third on the grid into the lead at the first corner and led a Ferrari 1-2 ahead of the 512M of Gary Pearson, until Hart spun at Brooklands handing the lead to Pearson who was closely hassled by the two Lola T70s of Martin O'Connell and Olly Bryant until the two Lolas dived past. With the pit stop window coinciding with a safety car the whole field came in for their mandatory pit stops with Callum Lockie in the diminutive Chevron B8 actually leading the field behind the safety car, which he rapidly lost at the restart! The yellow Ferrari 512M now driven by Alex Brundle took the win ahead of the Lola T70 of Olly Bryant.

Sunday's Big Cat Challenge saw the Pearson brothers take an early lead. Gary in first driving an E-Type he shared with Alex Brundle and John following in a car he would be handing over to Gary. After the pitstops Gary lead from Alex Brundle, whose car began to smoke in the slower corners, and that's how they finished (meaning that Gary Pearson took both the second and first steps on the podium.

Two races in one for the RAC Woodcote Trophy and Stirling Moss Trophy. Three Lotus 15s, driven by Andrew Kirkcaldy, Olly Bryant, and Roger Wills quickly broke away from the rest of the field led by Nigel Greensall's Lister Costin, until Tim Stamper's Aston Martin DB2/4 rolled at The Loop, bringing out the safety car for a couple of laps before the race was red-flagged. A rain shower during the stop meant the race restarted under the safety car on a wet track with Olly Bryant and Roger Wills out in front, in which positions they stayed to the flag. The Woodcote Trophy race was won by John and Gary Person in a short-nosed Jaguar D-Type.

The Transatlantic pre-1966 Touring Cars race saw pole sitter Sam Tordoff take the thundering Ford Falcon into the lead closely followed by the Mustangs of Nigel Greensall and Andy Priaulx, with Greensall taking the lead when Tordoff pitted. When all had made their pitstops the Greensall car, taken over by John Spiers was in the lead until with 10 minutes left to run Mike Whitaker pushed his Mustang to the front, with a hard charging Tordoff getting the Falcon back up to second.

With just six minutes left to run Whitaker's blew the diff on the entrance to Copse beaching the car in the gravel and laying down an oil slick, which brought out the safety car under which the race finished with Sam Tordoff's Ford Falcon taking the win from the Greensall/Spiers Ford Mustang.

Last race of the weekend, the HSCC Road Sports Trophy was interrupted when the Lotus Elan of John Dickson and the Datsun 260Z of John Hall came together at Club requiring a

lengthy safety car period to recover those cars and a number of others stopped trackside.

After the pit stops during the safety car period the lead was taken by Nigel Greensall who had taken over from Kevin Kivlochan in the open Shelby Cobra which he took a comfortable win at the finish from pole sitter John Davison in a Lotus Elan FHC.

PJO

DEREK BELL TROPHY FOR HSCC FORMULA LIBRE

With the engine of his newly-purchased Modus M1 having let go in Friday qualifying Henry Chart started from the back of the grid in this Trojan T101 after the Simon Hadfield Motorsport team returned to base and resurrected the Trojan overnight. Chart rewarded their hard work with a storming drive through the field to take the win in Saturday's race, and also triumphed in Sunday's running.

Trojan built customer cars for McLaren, including all of the McLaren Formula 5000 cars. With McLaren no longer willing to provide customer cars, Trojan produced their in-house designed T101 in 1973. The T101 proved incredibly successful on both sides of the Atlantic with Jody Scheckter taking the USA L&M Formula 500 Championship in a Sid Taylor entered T101, while in the UK T101s propelled Keith Holland, Brett Lunger, and Bob Evans to places in the top ten of the 1973 Rothmans Formula 5000 Championship.

DEREK BELL TROPHY FOR HSCC FORMULA LIBRE

Second and third place finishers in Sunday's Formula Libre race Christian Pittard, Chevron B28 (#51) and Paul Campfield, Chevron B24 (#30).

Only two Chevron B28s were built, both for the Belgian *Racing Team VDS* who had won the 1973 British Formula 5000 championship with a Chevron B24 driven by Teddy Pilette. Peter Gethin took the second spot in the 1974 championship with the B28. The VDS team also dominated the 1975 championship taking first and second spots, this time running Lola T400s for Pilette and Gethin.

Count Rudy van de Straten Ponthoz (of the Stella Artois brewing family) founded Racing Team VDS in 1964 initially racing a Mini Cooper then up to the peak of the team's success when Geoff Brabham won the 1981 Can-Am Challenge driving the VDS001, the teams' in-house development of their previously raced Lola T530.

MRL HISTORIC TOURING CAR CHALLENGE

From eleventh on the grid a delighted Wim Kuijl brought this 1975 Ford Capri home with a 42 second lead over the second place finisher, the Ford RS500 of Max and Ian Goff.

MRL HISTORIC TOURING CAR CHALLENGE

First lap and the two front row Ford RS500s of Paul Mensley/Michael Lyons (#22) and Julian Thomas/Calum Lockie (#101) are still together rounding a wet Copse corner watched by an appreciative grandstand audience. Neither car finished the race, only completing nine and seven laps respectively.

MASTERS RACING LEGENDS (FORMULA ONE 1966-1985}

The Shadow DN9 from 1979, driven by Mark Harrison, ahead of the 1983 Arrows A6 of Simon Fish.

Don Nicholls founded Advanced Vehicle Systems in California in 1968 to produce racing cars under the Shadow name, initially for the Can-Am Series with the innovative, quick, but unreliable Shadow Mk1 (*see page 92*).

Shadow moved into F1 in 1973 with sponsorship from UOP (United Oil Products), debuting at the South African GP with two Shadow DN1 cars for Jackie Oliver and George Fulmer. While Oliver DNF'd, Fulmer claimed sixth place. At the following race, in Spain, a second DN1 appeared for the Embassy Hill racing team driven by Graham Hill.

The DN9 was introduced in the 1978 season at the US GP West in Long Beach driven by Hans-Joachim Stuck for the factory team and Danny Ongais for Interscope Racing; with Clay Regazzoni getting the second works DN9 for the Monaco GP. Results were disappointing, the best being two fifth places for Stuck at the British GP and Regazzoni in Sweden. Stuck and Regazzoni were replaced for 1979 by Jan Lammers and Elio de Angelis but results were equally bad, with only De Angelis' fourth place at Watkins Glen lifting the team's gloom at the end of the season.

MASTERS RACING LEGENDS (FORMULA ONE 1966-1985)

This 1976 Wolf-Williams FW05 was driven by Yutaka Toriba at Silverstone in 2023.

By 1975 Frank Williams' eponymously named team (Frank Williams Racing Cars) was fast running out of money with little success to show. Canadian businessman Walter Wolf bought a 60% stake in the team while retaining Williams as Team Manager. Wolf also purchased the assets of the Hesketh team, including the Harvey Postelthwaite designed 308C car which James Hunt had driven in the 1975 Italian and USA GPs before Hesketh withdrew from Formula One.

The newly formed Wolf-Williams Racing hired Postlethwaite as chief engineer to improve the 308C which then became known as the Wolf-Williams FW05. Jacky Ickx was the team's initial lead driver during the 1976 season; but achieved limited success, and was fired after failing to qualify for the British GP, to be replaced by Arturo Merzario. After poor results for the rest of the season, Wolf removed Williams from his team manager position, prompting Williams to leave and set up Williams Grand Prix Engineering with Patrick Head.

Postlethwaite designed an all-new car for the 1977 season, the WR1, which Jody Scheckter would take to a debut win at the season opening Argentinian GP for the now renamed Walter Wolf Racing. Two more wins at Monaco and Canada would see Scheckter finish the season second in the drivers championship; but this was to be the highpoint for the team. Despite Postlethwaite designing new cars suitable for the ground-effect era, the lack of success led to Wolf selling the team assets to Emerson Fittipaldi at the end of the 1979 season.

HSCC THUNDERSPORTS

2023

Michael Lyons drove the IBEC 308LM to victory in the Thundersports race.

The IBEC 308 LM, later referred to as the IBEC P6, was designed by Harvey Postlethwaite for Lloyds insurance broker Ian Bracey to compete at Le Mans and used a lot of components from the Hesketh 308 F1 car including the Cosworth DFV 3 litre engine.

Entered for the 1978 24 Hours of Le Mans and driven by Ian Grob and Guy Edwards, with Bracey as reserve driver, the car lasted for 19 hours before the engine blew.

The team returned to Le Mans in 1980 with Tiff Needell and Tony Trimmer driving but failed to qualify. Needell and Trimmer shared driving duties again in 1981 but were out after 15 hours with another engine failure.

236

HSCC THUNDERSPORTS

Tim Brook drove this third generation (C3) 1969 Chevrolet Corvette in the Thundersports race.

Introduced in 1953, the Corvette has been in continuous production ever since with over 1.8 million cars made over all generations, and is widely known as "America's Sports Car", its popularity enhanced by its early connection with the TV series *Route 66*.

Just 300 Corvettes were hand-built in 1953, all featuring a fibreglass body available only in white with a red interior, and powered by a 3.9 litre inline six cylinder engine. Very basic with clip-in side windows, even interior door handles were an option! V8 engines were offered as an option in 1955, with the inline six discontinued in 1956.

International motorsport success came for the Corvette when Briggs Cunningham entered a team of three 4.6 litre Corvette C1 Coupés for the 1960 Le Mans 24 hours, driven by the driver pairings of Cunningham/Bill Kimberley, Dick Thompson/Fred Windridge, and John Fitch/Bob Grossman. A fourth C1 was entered by Lloyd 'Lucky' Casner's Camoradi USA team with Fred Gamble and Leon Lilley sharing driver duties.

The Fitch/Grossman car finished eighth on the road and took the winning laurels in the GT5.0 class. The Camoradi Corvette finished but was not classified having completed insufficient distance according to the organiser's arcane race rules.

HSCC THUNDERSPORTS

Ross Hyett drove this Lola T70 to third place in the Thundersports race.

Eric Broadley's design for the T70 was originally an open sports racer which gained early success in the USA with Walt Hansgen driving a Ford engined T70 entered by John Mecom to victory in the Monterey Grand Prix at Laguna Seca, California in 1965.

For the inaugural season of the Canadian-American Challenge Cup, (Can-Am), Lola T70s were all conquering winning all but the Laguna Seca race where Phil Hill's Chaparral 2E took the laurels. John Surtees' three victories gave him the title ahead of Mark Donohue in another T70.

The coupé version of the T70 had a singular success when the Penske Racing T70 MkIIIB driven by Mark Donohue and Chuck Parsons won the 1969 Daytona 24 hours, despite spending over an hour in the pits welding cracked exhaust pipes, after all the leading Porsche 908s retired with the same camshaft failure. Another T70 MkIII entered by actor James Garner's American International Racing Team and driven by Lothar Motschbacher and Ed Leslie came second.

2023

HSCC THUNDERSPORTS

David and Mike Smith raced the ex-Ross Hyett Blue Coral Porsche 935.

G Force Motorsport contested the BRDC National Sports GT Challenge (now the British GT Championship) in 1993 with two Blue Coral sponsored Porsche 935s driven by team founder John Greasley and Ross Hyett. Greasley finished first in Class A, with Hyett taking the second spot. The following year they reversed the places with Hyett first in class and Greasley second.

The Porsche 935 was the factory's racing version of the 911 made available in 1977 to customers racing in the World Championship of Makes, IMSA GT Championship and the DRM. Its best international result was at the 1979 Le Mans 24 Hours when the Kremer Racing 935-K3 driven by Klaus Ludwig, Don Whittington and Bill Whittington finished first overall, with the Dick Barbour Racing 935 of Barbour, Rolf Stommelen and Hollywood legend Paul Newman in second place.

2023

MRL BIG CAT CHALLENGE TROPHY

Gary Pearson finished both first and second having shared this winning E-Type (#27) with his brother John, and also the second placed E-Type (#23) with Alex Brundle. The E-type of John Clark (#18) follows into The Loop.

Enzo Ferrari supposedly described the Jaguar E-Type as "The most beautiful car ever made" on its introduction. Even without Ferrari's endorsement the combination of looks and performance ensured the E-Type was an instant sales success both in Europe and the USA, where it was known as the XK-E.

Although Jaguar never intended the E Type to be a race car, in the mould of the preceding C and D Types, just a month after its sensational debut at the 1961 Geneva Motor Show Graham Hill and Roy Salvadori drove two of the new E Types to first and third in the Oulton Park Trophy.

MRL BIG CAT CHALLENGE TROPHY

'Grace–Space–Pace' was Jaguar's advertising slogan back in the 1950s and 60s, and it applied particularly to the Jaguar Mk. 2 Saloon. Favoured by the police and bank robbers alike, the Mk. 2 quickly gained a reputation for its speed and handling coupled with room for the family (or bags of swag!).

Not too shabby on track either with famous examples being piloted by the likes of Jack Sears, Graham Hill and Mike Parkes who finished third, fourth and fifth respectively in the 1962 British Saloon Car Championship. Parkes and Jimmy Blumer also drove a Jaguar Mk.2 to victory in The Motor Six Hours International Saloon Car Race at Brands Hatch in October of that year.

Nick and Harry Whale shared the driving of this Mk.2 at the Silverstone Festival.

ADRIAN FLUX TROPHY FOR TRANSATLANTIC PRE 1966 TOURING CARS

Sam Tordof took this 1964 Ford Falcon Sprint from pole to a win at the flag.

Ford became the first of the big three USA manufacturers to market a 'compact' car with the introduction of the Falcon in 1960. In 1963 the Sprint variant was available with a 4.2 litre V8 engine, later a 4.8 litre, rather than the 2.4 litre straight six engine of the original models.

Its position as a 'performance' Ford was rather overshadowed by the introduction of the Ford Mustang which offered much the same, in a more sporty body style, for not much more money, and the Falcon Sprint was discontinued in 1965.

ADRIAN FLUX TROPHY FOR TRANSATLANTIC PRE 1966 TOURING CARS

The Steve Soper/Henry Mann Mustang (#7), which finished third, chased through Abbey by the similar car driven by Andy Priaulx and Alex Taylor who came home in fifth place.

As well as its successes on track the Mustang has also graced the silver screen with many appearances in feature films, most notably in *Bullitt* where Steve McQueen drives a 1968 Mustang GT fastback in probably the greatest car chase sequence of all time. The Mustang's first film appearance was, not as popularly believed in the James Bond film *Goldfinger,* but in the 1964 French comedy *Le Gendarme de Saint Tropez* where a poppy red convertible is driven by Geneviève Grad.

INTERNATIONAL TROPHY FOR CLASSIC GT CARS (pre 1966)

The 1961 Mark 2 TVR Grantura of Florian and Julius Brandt three-wheeling all the way around Luffield.

The Grantura was TVR's first production car which made its debut in 1958 as the Mark 1, with production continuing until the Mark 4 variant in 1967.

Hand built in TVR's Blackpool factory the glassfibre bodied Grantura could be specified with a number of different power units, including side valve or OHV Ford engines, a Coventry Climax engine, the 1600cc B Series engine from the MGA, or in later models the 1800 B Series from the MGB.

2023

INTERNATIONAL TROPHY FOR CLASSIC GT CARS (pre 1966)

Mini-based Ogle SX 1000 driven by Mark Burnett.

In the 1960s a number of Mini-based GT cars were produced, including the Mini Marcos and Unipower GT. Probably the best of these was the Ogle SX 1000 from the studio of industrial designer David Ogle. Due to BMC's refusal to supply Ogle with parts, the first customers had to take their own Mini to Ogle's factory to have the body cut off and replaced with the shapely fibreglass Ogle body at the cost of £500. BMC later relented and customers could then buy a complete SX 1000 for the princely sum of £1,176 12s 9d (equivalent to over £30,000 today!) A road test by Michael Tee in the October 1962 issue of *Motor Sport* praised the quality of the fibreglass bodywork; but stated: *"Economically it is difficult to justify the purchase of a car like this which is heavier than the standard car from which it is derived and has fewer seats."*

Fewer than 70 SX 1000s were made and production ceased after David Ogle died in May 1962 when the SX 1000 he was driving to Brands Hatch collided with a van on the A1.

MRL RAC WOODCOTE TROPHY & STIRLING MOSS TROPHY

1955 Jaguar D Type was driven by Ben Eastick to a solid mid-field finish.

After winning Le Mans in 1951 and 1953 with the C Type, Jaguar introduced the radically different D-Type for the 1954 race. Using a monocoque construction, rather than a tubular spaceframe chassis, and improved aerodynamics the three D-Types proved fast, reaching 173 mph on the Mulsanne straight; but were delayed by pit stops to counter fuel starvation, although the Duncan Hamilton/Tony Rolt car managed to finish second.

In 1955 Mike Hawthorn and Ivor Bueb scored the first Le Mans victory for the D Type. Hawthorn also won the Sebring 12 Hours race in a D Type entered by Briggs Cunningham that he shared with Phil Walters.

Jaguar entered three D Types for the 1956 Le Mans; but only one works car finished, while the Ecurie Ecosse D Type driven by Ron Flockhart and Ninian Sanderson won. Jaguar withdrew from racing at the end of that year; but in 1957 privately entered D Types took five of the top six places with the two Ecurie Ecosse cars taking first and second spots driven by Flockhart/Bueb and Sanderson/Lawrence respectively.

2023

HGPCA PRE 1966 GRAND PRIX CARS

The first race for Pre-66 GP cars saw two of the great marques of British motorsport from different eras as seen on this spread competing in the same race, that are both linked by one name — that of Raymond Mays.

Mays, a succesful racing driver in the 1920s and 1930s, was one of the founders of ERA (English Racing Automobiles) in 1933 and was the driving force behind the creation of BRM (British Racing Motors) after the war.

The ERA R3A is one of a series of ERA cars that competed with some success in the pre-war 'voiturette' class (a step down from the full-bore GP cars of the day) driven by, among others, Richard Seaman who later went on to drive for the Mercedes Benz GP team.

Mark Gillies is seen here hard at work behind the wheel of the R3A at Silverstone. The orange dot near the fuel filler shows that the car is running on ethanol, rather than regular petroleum.

2023

2023

HGPCA PRE 1966 GRAND PRIX CARS

After the disappointment of BRM's first car, the V16 engined P15 (*see page 252*), the team's results gradually improved; but it wasn't until 1959 that BRM scored its first World Championship race victory with Jo Bonnier winning that year's Dutch GP at Zandvort in the later, much simpler, (although still front-engined) 2.5 litre 4 cylinder P25. The early 1960s were a glorious period for BRM with Graham Hill winning his first driver's championship in 1962, and BRM taking the constructor's title the same year with the, now rear-engined, P57.

The P261, fitted with the BRM P65 1.5 litre V8 engine, showed outstanding promise on its race debut, the Daily Mirror Trophy race at Snetterton in March 1964. Graham Hill qualified the car second on the grid, but in atrocious conditions aquaplaned off into the bank early in the race.

The opening race of the 1964 F1 championship season at Monaco saw BRM works drivers Hill and Richie Ginther finish first and second at Monaco (the first of Hill's five wins at Monaco). At the end of the season Hill was second in the Driver's Championship and BRM took second spot in the Constructors Title.

For 1965 Hill was partnered with Jackie Stewart in BRM P261s. Hill placed the P261 on pole in four races, taking wins at Monaco (again) and the US GP at Watkins Glen, to repeat his second place standing in the drivers' title behind Jim Clark. Stewart's win at Monza helped secure BRM second in the constructors championship. Over that winter the P261s were fitted with 1.9 litre versions of the P65 engine to contest the Tasman Series in New Zealand and Australia, where Stewart and Hill took the first and second spots respectively.

Graham Adelman drove this BRM P261 at the Silverstone Festival.

2023

South Africa is not a country that springs to mind when thinking about Formula One constructors; but there were actually two (LDS, run by Doug Saurier, that built a number of cars based on Coopers and Brabhams, and this pretty little Assegai. Designed and built by South African racing driver Tony Kotzé it drew visual inspiration from the 'Sharknose' Ferrari 156 and used a 1.5 litre Alfa Romeo engine.

Praised for its outstanding build quality, the performance sadly didn't match up and Kotzé failed to qualify the car for its one and only F1 appearance at the non-Championship Rand Grand Prix at Kyalami in 1962.

The car was purchased by John Carpenter in 2015 and returned to its original 1962 Kyalami spec by Iain Rowley's Delta Motorsport. Its maiden appearance on the Historic racing scene was at the 2016 Monaco Historic GP where Rowley drove it a solid mid-field finish.

The Assegai is currently owned by Julian Ellison seen here driving the car at Silverstone in 2023.

HGPCA PRE 1966 GRAND PRIX CARS

Another F1 oddity from the early 1960s is this Walker Special. Designed and built by Alf Francis, Stirling Moss' long time racing mechanic and chief mechanic for the Rob Walker Racing Team, as Rob Walker was considering manufacturing his own car in 1960 rather than using other manufacturer's cars for his privateer team.

Using a 2.5 litre Coventry Climax engine the project was abandoned when the F1 regulations changed to 1.5 litres for the 1961 season and Walker continued entering a Lotus 18 for Stirling Moss, with Moss taking a memorable win at the first race of the season in Monaco.

The Walker Special was driven at Silverstone by Russell McCarthy.

BRM P15 1.5 LITRE V16 (RECREATION)

After the Second World War Raymond Mays was instrumental in getting together a consortium of British motor industrialists, including Oliver Lucas, Alfred Owen, Tony Vandervell and David Brown, to support the foundation of BRM (British Racing Motors).

BRM's first car, the over-complicated 1.5 litre V16 engined P15, suffered from reliability problems, failing on its first appearance at Silverstone in August 1950 when it broke a driveshaft at the start in the non-championship International Trophy race. No such problem for this Hall & Hall recreation of the P15 at Silverstone in 2023 demonstrated by Rob Hall who gets a touch of opposite lock on through Club corner.

The P15's second appearance, at a very wet Goodwood a month later, yielded a much better result with Reg Parnell winning the non-championship Goodwood Trophy F1 race. In 1951 BRM managed only two appearances including the British GP where Parnell and Peter Walker started from the back of the grid because the team arrived late and neither car practised nor qualified. After an heroic drive they finished seventh and eight despite both drivers suffering burns to hands and feet.

However, with Alfa Romeo withdrawing from F1 the 1952 and 1953 World Championship was run to Formula 2 regulations, leaving the P15 only eligible for Formula Libre and non-championship F1 events. Juan Manuel Fangio scored some notable wins in the car including at the non-championship Albi Grand Prix in 1953, with Ken Wharton second in another P15.

2023

MERCEDES F1 W04 (2013)

Esteban Gutierrez was clearly enjoying himself demonstrating the Mercedes W04 from 2013, the year that 2008 World Champion Lewis Hamilton moved from McLaren to join Nico Rosberg in the Mercedes Team, replacing Michael Schumacher who retired (for the second time) at the end of the 2012 season.

Rosberg and Hamilton locked out the front row of the grid for two consecutive races in Spain and Monaco, with Rosberg scoring the W04's first win at Monaco. Further wins at the British (Rosberg) and Hungarian (Hamilton) GPs helped secure second spot in the 2013 constructor's championship for Mercedes.

Race 1: Historic Formula Junior
First: *Sam Wilson (Lotus 20/22)*
Second: *Alex Ames (Brabham BT6)*
Third: *Samuel Harrison (Rennmax BN1-2)*

Race 2: HSCC Thundersports
First: *Michael Lyons (Ibec 308LM)*
Second: *Dan Eagling (Royale RP17)*
Third: *Ross Hyett (Lola T70 Mk3B)*

Race 3: Derek Bell Trophy for HSCC Formula Libre
First: *Henry Chart (Trojan T101)*
Second: *Andy Smith (March 782)*
Third: *Christian Pettard (Chevron B28)*

Race 4: MRL Historic Touring Car Challenge
First: *Wim Kuijl (Ford Capri)'*
Second: *Goff M / Goff I (Ford Sierra Cosworth RS500)*
Third: *Ric Wood (Nissan Skyline GT-R)*

Race 5: Masters Racing Legends (Formula One 1966-1985)
First: *Ken Tyrrell (Tyrrell 011)*
Second: *Steve Hartley (McLaren MP4/1)*
Third: *Martin Stretton (Tyrrell 012)*

Race 6: Masters GT Trophy
First: *Craig Wilkins (Lamborghini Huracan Super Trofeo Evo)*
Second: *Whight / Mackinnon (Aston Martin Vantage GT2)*
Third: *Jason McInulty (Lamborghini Huracan Super Trofeo Evo)*

Race 7: HGPCA Pre 1966 Grand Prix Cars
First: *Charlie Martin (Cooper T53)*
Second: *Nick Fennell (Lotus 25)*
Third: *Tim Child (Brabham BT3/4)*

Race 8: International Trophy for Classic GT Cars (Pre 1966)
First: *Thomas/Lockie (Shelby American Cobra Daytona)*
Second: *Greensell / Spiers(TVR Griffith)*
Third: *Mike Whitaker (TVR Griffith)*

Race 9: Masters Endurance Legends
First: *Steve Brooks (Peugeot 90X)*
Second: *Harinda De Silva / Tim De Silva (Peugeot LMP1)*
Third: *Stuart Wiltshire (Peugeot 90X*

Race 10: Yokohama Trophy for Masters Sports Car Legends
First: *Garry Pearson / Alex Brundle (Ferrari 512M)*
Second: *Oliver Bryant (Lola T70 Mk3B)*
Third: *Claridge / Gomes (Lola T296)*

Race 11: Historic Formula Junior
First: *Sam Wilson (Lotus 20/22)*
Second: *Horatio Fitz-Simon (Lotus 22)*
Third: *Alex Ames (Brabham BT6)*

Race 12: MRL Big Cat Trophy
First: *John Pearson / Garry Pearson (Jaguar E-Type)*
Second: *Garry Pearson / Alex Brundle (Jaguar E-Type)*
Third: *Thorpe / Quaife (Jaguar E-Type)*

MRL HISTORIC TOURING CAR CHALLENGE

The Richard Kent/Joe Osborne Broadspeed Capri (#88) chases the Andy Wolfe/Darren Turner RS3100 Capri (#63) out of a very damp Copse corner on the first lap. Neither car would finish the race.

Race 13: Derek Bell Trophy for HSCC Formula Libre
First: Henry Chart (Trojan T101)
Second: Christian Pettard (Chevron B28)
Third: Paul Campfield (Chevron B24)

Race 14: MRL Royal Automobile Club Woodcote Trophy & Stirling Moss Trophy
First: Oliver Bryant (Lotus 15)
Second: Roger Wills (Lotus 15)
Third: Spiers / Greensall (Lister Knobbly)

Race 15: Masters Racing Legends (Formula One 1966-1985)
First: Michael Lyons (Lotus 92)
Second: Martin Stretton (Tyrrell 012)
Third: Ken Tyrrell (Tyrrell 011)

Race 16: 75th Anniversary Trophy for HGPCA Front-Engined Grand Prix Cars (1948-1960)
First: Mark Shaw (Scarab Offenhauser)
Second: John Spiers (Maserati 250F)
Third: Rod Jolley (Lister Jaguar Monza GP)

Race 17: Adrian Flux Trophy for Transatlantic pre-1966 Touring Cars
First: Sam Tordoff (Ford Falcon Sprint)
Second: Greensall / Spiers (Ford Mustang)
Third: Soper / Mann (Ford Mustang)

Race 18: HGPCA pre-1966 Grand Prix Cars (Rear Engined)
First: Charlie Martin (Cooper T5)
Second: Tim Child (Brabham BT3/4)
Third: Sam Wilson (Cooper T53)

Race 19: Masters Endurance Legends
First: Steve Brooks (Peugeot 90X)
Second: Stuart Wiltshire (Peugeot 90X)
Third: Christophe D'Ansembourg (Lola Aston DBR1-2)

Race 20: HSCC Road Sports Trophy
First: Kivlochan / Greensall (Shelby Cobra)
Second: John Davison (Lotus Elan S1)
Third: Simon King (Morgan Plus 8)